TRANSITIONS
IN
WORSHIP

TRANSITIONS IN WORSHIP

*Moving from
Traditional to
Contemporary*

ANDY LANGFORD

Abingdon Press
Nashville

TRANSITIONS IN WORSHIP:
MOVING FROM TRADITIONAL TO CONTEMPORARY

Copyright © 1999 by Abingdon Press

This book is printed on acid-free paper.

Library of Congress Cataloging-in-Publication Data

Langford, Andy.
   Transitions in worship : moving from traditional to contemporary / Andy Langford.
      p.   cm.
   Includes bibliographical references.
   ISBN 0-687-08173-4 (pbk. : alk. paper)
   1. United Methodist Church (U.S.)—Liturgy.   2. Public worship—United Methodist Church (U.S.)   3. Church renewal—United Methodist Church (U.S.) 4. Methodist Church—Liturgy.   I. Title.
BX8382.Z5L36   1999
264'.076—dc21   98-35786
                                                                                      CIP

Scripture quotations, unless otherwise indicated, are from the New Revised Standard Version Bible, copyright © 1989, by the Division of Christian Education of the National Council of the Churches of Christ in the United States of America.

Portions of Appendix 1 have been adapted from *Contemporary Worship for the 21st Century: Worship or Evangelism?* by Daniel T. Benedict and Craig K. Miller. © 1994 by Discipleship Resources, Nashville, TN.

99 00 01 02 03 04 05 06 07 08—10 9 8 7 6 5 4 3 2 1

MANUFACTURED IN THE UNITED STATES OF AMERICA

CONTENTS

INTRODUCTION

The advertisement grabbed readers' attention. Flyers distributed to local residents invited people to "Meet a Modern Hero":

> He advocated women's rights in a time of crushing patriarchalism. He sanctioned peacemaking and blessed those who were hungry and thirsty for righteousness. He healed those sick in mind and body with a simple touch. He was scorned, abused, and murdered for his outrageous ideas about God. He gave his life for his friends.[1]

The flyer announced a new service of worship. The gathering would be Saturday evening in a community garden, with the worship led from an electronic keyboard played by a casually dressed musician. A large quilt filled with a brilliant cross would be the only religious symbol. The teaching would be conversational. And people came. So began a contemporary worship service at Belmont United Methodist Church in Nashville.

Today, congregations of Christians throughout North America and the world are experimenting with new patterns and styles of worship. Many congregations seek to serve their current members, especially younger people who want "something more" or "something less formal" or "something that feels different." Other churches are reaching out to persons who have been alienated from Christianity or have become inactive because they are dissatisfied with current worship practices. Even more significantly, an increasing number of congregations are reaching out to people in their communities who have no religious background or are unconnected to the Christian faith, yet who are seeking answers to life's questions. Ministry to new generations, the alienated, and the unchurched has initiated significant worship changes: Saturday night supplants Sunday morning, stools take the place of pulpits, sports shirts dislodge clerical robes, choruses replace hymns, synthesizers substitute for organs, and new worship leaders emerge.

These and numerous other changes in worship, nevertheless, pose many key questions to the church and those persons who lead worship. What is contemporary worship? Where did it come from? What are its problems? What theology does it reflect? What are its implications for established services and congregations? How may congregations respond?

Quick answers to these questions are typically wrong. Some observers of contemporary worship make hasty judgments about new forms of worship and say, "It's just a fad." Because some new patterns of worship appear radically alien, a number of commentators declare, "It has style but no substance." Other worship leaders simply want quick solutions to increase worship attendance: "Give me the three best changes that will reach baby boomers" or "What are the best contemporary choruses to sing?"

Before congregations and worship leaders jump on the contemporary bandwagon, turn their backs on new forms and styles of worship, or make any quick judgments and decisions about emerging worship trends, they should read this book, which provides an overview of contemporary worship. Written for pastors, musicians, and other worship leaders in local congregations, this book surveys where worship has been, where it is now, and where it might be going.

The outline of the book responds to these questions. Chapter 1 describes three primary patterns of contemporary worship: Liturgical, Praise and Worship, and Seeker services. These categories define the present worship landscape. Chapter 2 places these three styles within the context of recent mainline denominational liturgical reform, as well as distinctly nontraditional worship models. Contemporary worship is an extension of the liturgical reform movement, yet also stands in tension with most leaders of that very tradition. Chapter 3 describes the primary influence that has led to changing worship patterns: conflicting sensibilities among contemporary generations of Christian believers and unchurched seekers. The changing demographics of North American culture have created an entirely new context of worship. Chapter 4 raises the central theological question posed by contemporary worship: Why do we worship? This theological question must be answered, and its answer reflects a fundamental debate among Christian theologians. The focus then shifts to specific suggestions for an established church wanting to make its worship more attuned to new generations. Chapter 5 outlines the four foundation stones of worship: the Word of God, the sacraments, prayer, and fellowship. Without these four blocks, worship will fail. Chapter 6 describes the first four things any congregation must do if it wishes to strengthen worship: create a worship team, ask the right questions, create a vision, and name an audience. Changes in worship without such first steps will fail. Finally, chapter 7 offers two specific ways for established congregations to serve younger generations, the alienated, and seekers more effectively: starting a new service and blending together elements from all three worship styles. All of this information is crucial for leaders and congregations deciding how to worship in the contemporary world.

This book reflects my own liturgical journey. I grew up in a United Methodist congregation in Durham, North Carolina, that featured traditional Protestant worship. Stained-glass windows surrounded the congregation as we gathered in a pulpit-centered sanctuary. The congregation, dressed in Sunday clothes, was Anglo, middle class, and full of married couples with numerous children. A large choir in robes sat behind the pulpit, and a pipe organ led the music. Our pastors wore black robes and began worship by kneeling in private prayer in front of the congregation. Vested acolytes processed in to light the candles during a choral call to worship, and the congregation recited the Apostles' Creed, Gloria Patri, Doxology (to the tune of OLD 100th), and the Lord's Prayer every Sunday from memory. The heart of the service was the sermon, indicated by the dimming of the sanctuary lights and the lighting of a spotlight on the pulpit. In that place and through that worship I was formed and shaped by the gospel. Despite my profound appreciation of this style of liturgy, however, I understand how today such worship is for many people anachronistic. It served past generations well and is a worship style that many still revere, but for a number of people in newer generations it reflects an alien culture that is rapidly disappearing.

As I grew in my faith and prepared for Christian ministry, I discovered even richer styles of worship. From liturgical scholars, I grew in my appreciation of historic liturgical theology and practice from the Eastern and Western church: the Christian year, a high view of the sacraments, the lectionary, and classic rites and rituals. Through most of my professional life, I have served as a proponent and leader of such classic liturgical worship.

Today, I am more inclusive. While I still appreciate the worship in which I was raised and trained, and worship such as that found in Westminster Abby in London deeply feeds my soul, I am increasingly enthusiastic about radically new patterns and styles of worship that reach whole new cultures for Christ.

My moment of epiphany, when I saw that the worship that formed me as a child and adult required serious reform, occurred some ten years ago. I was attending an ecumenical meeting of liturgical scholars in San Francisco. On Sunday morning, an Episcopalian, a Presbyterian, and I attended Glide Memorial United Methodist Church in downtown San Francisco. The church building looked much like its neighborhood, an area called the Tenderloin District. Within this area of San Francisco, every kind of human flesh was for sale. Prostitutes, male and female, sold their bodies in front of the church; drug addicts huddled in the church doorways; flashing neon lights, advertising X-rated video stores and live sex shows, bounced off the exterior walls of the church. When we entered the building, men and women in rough blue jeans greeted us. The sanctuary was large enough to hold about one thousand people. Plywood covered the stained-glass windows. Banners made with flannel and glue, filled with words such as *hope*, *integrity, joy, peace*, and *respect*, hung on the walls. Multicolored strobe lights beamed down from the balcony.

What was most remarkable about Glide Memorial was the congregation itself. Some older persons wore traditional Sunday clothing: nice dresses or suits with ties. But these well-dressed people were the exception. Most of the people in the congregation clearly lived immediately around the church. Most people came in separately and sat alone. Some of the women and men, at least from what they wore, appeared to be prostitutes. Other men and women had a dazed, lost look on their faces, while other folk simply looked exhausted. Far too many of the people were young, but looked old beyond their years with listless eyes and thin bodies. By the time worship began, this mixed collection of people filled the sanctuary.

The pastor, Cecil Williams, entered wearing an African kente-cloth robe of brown, red, black, and green stripes. A band with drums, guitars, synthesizers, and horns warmed up on stage. Worship began. We had no bulletins and simply followed oral instructions. Having no hymnals, we sang along with the choir. The choir consisted of members of the congregation who came forward at various times and sat on the front steps of the stage. Extemporaneous prayers were offered, and many in the congregation called out prayer requests: to rid someone of drugs, to cure a friend with AIDS, or to feed the hungry. No Bible was ever opened during worship, although Scripture was quoted during the sermon. The unorthodox sermon was energetic and direct. Williams, walking among the congregation, told the people that no matter what society thought about them, God loved them. He declared that God did not make trash, and that God did not own a trash can. Williams urged the people to respect and love themselves. At the close of the service, the pastor did not invite us to partake of Holy Communion, but to come to the soup kitchen in the fellowship hall.

The two friends who attended worship with me were appalled. Both of them, excellent liturgical scholars, thought the sanctuary shabby, the lack of an organ troublesome, and the absence of a traditional sermon and classic hymns inhibiting to their worship. They found the service a waste of time. My worship colleagues were partially correct. By classic liturgical standards, Glide Memorial's worship broke every rule.

I felt differently, however; in Wesleyan language, my heart was "strangely warmed." Look at who came to worship! These people who, by their own actions or by the actions of others, were the trash of our society. Society's scavengers picked over their ragged and distorted souls. Yet, these people walked into Glide Memorial to hear good news. They did not have to come into the building and could have stayed on the streets, but they were hungry for affirmation and yearning for hope. That church, faithful to its mission, proclaimed God's love. Almost every other church in the area had fled to the suburbs or closed. Glide Memorial remained as a light in the midst of the darkness.

This congregation was serving its neighbors with a concrete mission. This community of faith accepted its neighbors as they were and attempted to meet their actual needs through media they could appreciate. Through its sanctuary, its music, its preaching, and its visuals, Glide Memorial shared the good news with those people who most wanted and needed to hear the message of love in worship.

The gospel has always been communicated through such indigenous worship—native to one particular people in one specific time and unique culture. When Jesus taught outdoors or in private homes or in the courtyard of the temple, crowds of people came to hear him. Jesus offended the righteous worship leaders, who worshiped in proper Jewish ways in synagogues and the temple, because the seekers and outcasts of their society came out whenever Jesus appeared and apparently understood his message. As Jesus said to the religious ones: "Truly, I tell you, the tax collectors and prostitutes are going into the kingdom of God ahead of you" (Matthew 21:31). The money-grabbers and the prostitutes, who appeared to the religious believers to have rejected God and would never darken the door of a synagogue, eagerly came to hear Jesus speak when he spoke of God's love in ways that they could understand.

My worship colleagues in San Francisco were good people, but on that day they were unable to appreciate this particular embodiment of the message of Jesus: God seeks and loves everyone. My friends forgot how Jesus communicated the gospel message in unconventional ways that spoke to distinct and frequently neglected audiences. The religious leaders in the temple and synagogues were good people, but they rejected the fact that the good news was for everyone and that there is more than one way to communicate God's grace. I began asking myself much more intently, What are the appropriate ways to share God's love through worship?

This question must be answered because of the contemporary cultural context. While many Christians now worship in established congregations, there are many more people outside these congregations who are seeking and needing God.

Currently in North America there are tens of millions of people who are looking for meaning in their lives. The majority of these seekers are under fifty years of age. They are very much like the seekers, the tax collectors, and the outcasts who came to see Jesus and those people in San Francisco who go to Glide Memorial. These searchers for God have different lifestyles. While some grew up in the church, the majority did not grow up going to worship and do not know the Bible, the Lord's Prayer, classic hymns, or any doxology. Many of these unchurched people, like many folk within the church, have been and still are self-centered. They have tried self-help, self-fulfillment, Eastern gurus, and financial consultants, and their lives are still incomplete. These people outside established congregations are searching for meaning, and they wonder if the church has an answer.

The church's answer is proclaimed and discovered in worship. Through the space and environment, music, sermon, visuals, actions, and every other aspect of worship, every Christian congregation primarily either reaches out or shuts its doors. Every congregation identifies principally with religious rulers in the temple or synagogues or with outsiders searching for God.

Glide Memorial forced me to ask, What are we doing in our worship? Has loyalty to one pattern or style of worship blinded the church to the missional task of worship to share the good news? Are there other ways to share the gospel than those now offered by many established congregations? There are no easy answers; but some answers may be found by more clearly identifying how and why Christians worship God today.

Annie Dillard, an author and Christian mystic, has written that worship contains tremendous power to transform lives. Too often, we in the church simply walk through our worship without understanding its divine energy to change women, men, youth, and children. As Dillard wrote:

> I do not find Christians, outside of the catacombs, sufficiently sensible of conditions. Does anyone have the foggiest idea what sort of power we so blithely invoke? Or, as I suspect, does no one believe a word of it? The churches are children playing on the floor with their chemistry sets, mixing up a batch of TNT to kill a Sunday morning.[2]

Today, congregations in North America face a profoundly unchristian culture. Yet, this culture still seeks a foundation that the church alone can provide. The task before the church is whether it will use the power of God's grace through worship to explode within our society the love of Jesus Christ.

1 | THREE PATTERNS OF CONTEMPORARY WORSHIP

O pen the Saturday newspaper in any community and look at the variety of worship services. In a large, urban newspaper, a Roman Catholic church lists half a dozen masses at different times and in different languages, and quite possibly one service with a mariachi band. An Assembly of God congregation offers three praise services, one of which features a special singing group. An Episcopal parish describes an early Morning Prayer service, followed by Holy Eucharist, while across the street an Orthodox Anglican Church in America rival offers worship using the service of the 1928 Prayerbook. A newly established Orthodox Church in America congregation promotes an "ancient orthodox liturgy in a modern tongue," while a Pentecostal Holiness church announces "Worship Filled with the Spirit." An African American community church describes worship out of the "Black Experience," and a Metropolitan Community Church "proudly serves the gay and lesbian community." And the listings continue. Is there one normative style of Christian worship in modern North America?

As has been the case historically, there is a rich variety of patterns and styles of Christian worship.[1] While twenty years ago, some observers identified the major North

American Christian worship options as Protestant and Roman Catholic, with a smattering of Oriental, Pentecostal, and Orthodox options, these categories are now far too simplistic.

Worship has always changed "as people and the needs of people have changed" and thus many worship traditions exist today.[2] Classically, there were seven major liturgical traditions (identified with their area of origin or author): Alexandrian, Western Syrian, Eastern Syrian, Basilian, Byzantine, Roman, and Gallic. Each of these liturgical traditions had and has its own distinctive contours and emphases. To add greater complexity, each of these traditions has liturgical variations. For example, while there is only one normative Roman Catholic ritual (written in Latin), different Roman Catholic language groups around the globe have instituted a host of regional variations.

The variety in worship becomes even more complex among Protestant traditions. Among Protestants, as liturgist James White has observed, "the richness of Protestant worship consists in its diversity and its consequent ability to serve a wide variety of peoples."[3] There are at least nine Protestant traditions—Anabaptist, Reformed, Anglican, Lutheran, Quaker, Puritan, Methodist, Frontier, and Pentecostal. Liturgical variety, often associated with different cultures or periods of time, is the Christian tradition.

Despite all the denominational and confessional differences, within North American culture there is a new way of defining worship. Overlapping old schemes and categorizations, the new pattern describes three primary patterns of contemporary worship: Liturgical, Praise and Worship, and Seeker.[4] See appendix 1 for a comparative outline of these three patterns. While other ways of categorizing worship exist, such as participation, performance, and entertainment styles or low church and high church categories or racial/ethnic expressions of worship, these three options are a useful way to categorize contemporary worship.[5]

While none of the three patterns exists in a perfect form in any congregation or fits any of the classic categories neatly, nevertheless the three are helpful descriptions or typologies for interpreting contemporary worship. These three patterns of worship exist in relationship and tension with one another, and each can be an authentic expression of the Christian faith. Each alternative pattern is contemporary, that is, the worship can presently be found in active congregations. Each pattern has strengths and weaknesses as a distinctive response to a particular group of persons. While each of the three speaks to and bonds together a specific group of people, each of them also excludes and sounds incomprehensible to other groups. A local congregation may worship predominantly in only one pattern, or in all three patterns at different services, or in a combination of the three. No one of these patterns of worship is necessarily better than the others; there is no one normative form of worship. A discussion of each of these three patterns helps clarify where the church currently stands in its worship.

Liturgical Worship

Liturgical worship is God-centered worship that at its best creates a sense of awe. Duke Chapel, in Durham, North Carolina, features Liturgical worship. The architecture is Gothic, with stone walls and floors, hard pews, and pew racks with hymnals. Members of the congregation carefully follow a printed order of worship, which includes printed prayers and directions for participating in worship. Vested choir members and worship leaders, led by a crucifer and acolytes, begin worship with a processional hymn and walk down a long center aisle to a divided chancel and choir stalls. Organs at both the front and rear of the chapel accompany the singing. The readings come from the lectionary—a calendar of the Christian year and a three-year

table of scripture readings for each Sunday and holy day—
and Holy Communion is a regular part of worship. The
preaching is theologically rich and addresses concretely
the needs of a highly educated but skeptical postmodern
community. Duke Chapel is full of students, faculty, and
residents of the area every Sunday morning.

Liturgical worship tends to be formal. The goal of worship is hearing and seeing the Word in rational and reasonable ways, and toward that end—based on its Old Eng-
lish word origin "weorth-scipe"—to honor or esteem the
wholly other God. Grounded on the lectionary and specific liturgical texts, Baptism and Holy Communion stand
at the heart of the community's life. Authorized prayerbooks, such as *The United Methodist Hymnal* and *The United
Methodist Book of Worship* are normative. Mainline Protestant churches, such as United Methodist, Presbyterian,
United Church of Christ, Episcopal, and Lutheran churches,
along with Roman Catholic and Orthodox congregations,
are the primary bastions of Liturgical services.

Liturgical worship's primary audience is the churched
believer who accepts, or is willing to struggle with, the
received faith. These persons may be members or visitors,
but most of them grew up in church. There are generally
more women than men, and the worshipers are usually
older rather than younger. Those members who are young
tend to be more educated than the population as a whole
and to have been raised within a Christian family. New
members most often transfer in from other Liturgical congregations. The members feel comfortable in a traditional
religious setting within a sanctuary with a pulpit, font,
table, and pews parallel to one another and the table/altar.
Services take place primarily on Sunday mornings with
printed worship bulletins that reference a hymnal or book
of worship. The congregation participates through singing
hymns and reading aloud printed prayers. The primary
human concerns of these people, and their worship lead-

ers, are human sin and the need for atoning grace, spoken about in overtly theological language. While outwardly these people appear to have made it, many understand themselves to be distant from God and are looking for good news. Pastors, music leaders, and choirs lead the service, often in ways that do not call attention to themselves. These worship leaders serve as presiders, who point away from themselves to God as they guide the community at prayer.

The particular evangelistic task, or the central goal, of the Liturgical service is distinctly different from that of Praise and Worship or Seeker services. The total evangelistic task of worship may be described as a three-stage process from introducing seekers to Jesus to inviting new hearers into community and then ultimately incorporating believers fully into Christ's ministry. Descriptively, this process is like steps leading to a porch that then leads into a house. Whereas Seeker services are basic introductions to God (the steps), and Praise and Worship teaches new converts (the porch) who then are baptized (the door), Liturgical services nurture and strengthen believers (who live within the household of God).[6]

Within this evangelistic process, the role of the Liturgical service is to provide a house for believers where sanctifying grace is offered and the Word and sacraments are rightly taught and practiced. The goal is to teach already committed followers of Jesus how to develop and strengthen their established faith. Because of the increasingly marginal character of churched believers and theological language in contemporary culture, Liturgical services sometimes stand as countercultural to a materialistic and narcissistic North American society.

Word and Table describes the shape of the Liturgical service. The service begins with an Entrance where the people gather. Next comes the Proclamation of the Word, usually including three readings from the lectionary plus one psalm. Preaching on the lectionary texts, pastors explain the readings for the day. Often, the preaching prepares the people to move to the table/altar or font. Sermons may be read from a manuscript or given without notes. The goal of preaching, as was often stated in preaching manuals of earlier generations, is to encourage people to go home and discuss the sermon over lunch. This educational model reflects a Platonic way of knowing: people become what they hear and subsequently think; if persons think the right thoughts they will become good people. Following the sermon come responses such as a historic creed. Thanksgiving with Holy Communion is the archetypal response to the Word, followed by the Sending Forth into service in the world. This basic pattern, followed every week, provides a comfort zone that establishes the boundaries for faithful worship.

Traditional music dominates Liturgical services. The choir and congregation sing hymns such as "Joyful, Joyful We Adore Thee" slowly and methodically. Organ and piano accompany the singing, while hymnals provide musical notes and words. The music may be magnificent or very simple, most often depending on the skill of the musicians. The choir may be polished or informal. The musical instruments may be of high quality, such as large tracker organs, or low quality, such as older electronic pianos.

Liturgical worship, despite its emphasis on building up believers, is not antithetical to incorporating new believers into the church. Every mainline denomination is attempting to reach new generations with disciplined patterns of incorporation, leading persons deeper into a spiritual life. Most of these patterns are based on the groundbreaking Roman Catholic Rite of Christian Initiation for Adults, which prepares the unchurched for baptism. Lutherans, Episcopalians, and United Methodists now are developing similar models of distinct rituals that bring persons into the church through several years of serious study. The difficulty is that each of these models of incorporation still attempts to bring seekers and new hearers into the language base, beliefs, and practices of established believers without enough cultural adaptation.[7]

Not every Liturgical service looks like every other Liturgical service. The degrees of formality range widely from small-membership country chapels to large-membership, high-steeple urban monuments. Variables include the frequency of Holy Communion (from several times a year to weekly), and the length of worship bulletins (from one page to multiple pages). A primary characteristic of a Liturgical service is that a congregation uses a printed worship bulletin (or a worship pattern imprinted in the mind of each worshiper in the case of Orthodox traditions) that follows the same basic pattern each week.

A variation of the Liturgical service, which some observers contend is a completely different category, is the Preaching service. This service of the Word, often understood as the traditional Protestant service, is a low church variation of the Word and Table pattern. These Protestant liturgies emerged in the late nineteenth century as North American Protestant congregations tried to imitate an Anglican worship pattern of Morning Prayer followed by a preaching service. These services emphasize the centrality of the scriptural Word and personal experience of God. This liturgy begins with a time of preparation that contains Scripture readings, prayer, the offering, and ministry announcements. The music consists of gospel songs and hymns accompanied by a piano or organ. Following these "preliminaries," the highlight of the service is the sermon—originally intended to be, but increasingly less of, an exposition of Scripture—by the worship leader, who is often called "Preacher." At the end of the sermon, during the closing hymn, the preacher invites people to be followers of Jesus Christ. These services are still widespread in many established Protestant churches, especially in the Sunbelt.

They are, however, a part of the Liturgical pattern in that the same outline is followed every week, worship bulletins guide the service, and traditional hymnody defines the music.

Liturgical services have value in current North American culture. They maintain an orthodox faith in a culture with few absolutes. Such worship respects a variety of past traditions and through the lectionary generally offers a more holistic reading of the Scripture. By their sacramental emphasis, even as persons are invited to enact their faith, these services remind persons that God is the primary actor in salvation. The music is rich and has stood the test of time. For faithful believers, Liturgical worship enables growth in grace.

Unfortunately, in too many Liturgical congregations tradition, habit, and social status are often more important than the liturgy itself. Ruled by the tyranny of tradition, the smell most often associated with Liturgical worship is not incense but mold and mildew. Frequently, Liturgical services are captive to particular regional traditions such as a mandated altar call or a particular style of dress. For example, clerical clothing is often based on a specific model, such as a Geneva academic gown or a Roman alb, and little variation is allowed. Many such services resist change; people declare, "We've never done this before!" Liturgical services often forget that every tradition arose as a response to a specific cultural context and explicit pastoral concern. For example, the creation of communion rails centuries ago was to prevent stray animals who wandered into open cathedrals from consuming the bread and cup; these rails have now become sacred objects upon which children (possibly in the minds of some people the modern equivalent of stray animals) must not play.

Liturgical services also suffer in that they often are too textual, too linear, too inbred, too pessimistic, and oblivious to current culture. Dependent on written texts, these services appear to be a checklist of necessary elements that must be repeated every week. Such services speak best to believers who are trained for worship by persons who have been previously nurtured by this very form; only the informed know which book to use at which point in the service. Liturgical worship's audience thus perpetuates itself and excludes persons who have not shared in this formation. Critics and supporters both observe that Liturgical services often lack a warm experiential expression and emphasize sin to make people feel guilty. Finally, Liturgical worship appears hostile to unchurched seekers when the worshipers sing hymns from long ago and speak of concerns not relevant to a local community.

Praise and Worship

Praise and Worship is a second alternative in contemporary worship. Belmont Church, an independent congregation in Nashville, Tennessee, has one such service. The worship begins at 10:00 A.M. as worshipers gather. In the lobby, hosts serve coffee, which may be taken into the auditorium, where persons sit in comfortable pews in a semicircle. No worship bulletins or hymnals are evident, but many people carry Bibles in leather covers. When still only a few people have arrived, worship begins as a worship leader mounts the central stage and begins playing a grand piano. A screen descends from the ceiling and the growing congregation sings scriptural choruses. After forty-five minutes of singing and extemporaneous prayer, the congregation numbers around one thousand people. The musician begins to slow down and soften the music and then leaves the stage. A teacher with black Bible in hand mounts the steps and teaches from a whole chapter of the Bible. After forty-five minutes of teaching, the teacher sits, and ushers pass offering baskets and communion plates from row to row, without the congregation being told what the baskets or bread and cups are about. Following the offering and distribution of the communion elements, the worship leader again guides singing as people begin to recess and visit with one another.

Praise and Worship services appear informal, focus on one topic or theme each Sunday, and present the gospel in an oral and musical style. Such worship most often uses praise chorus books or choruses projected on a screen in front of the congregation. The services feel modern and appeal to the emotions by focusing on the heart and feelings. The atmosphere seems like a festival in the park, and worship is the center of the congregation's life.

Based on contemporary musical sounds and experiences, Praise and Worship services are often found in evangelical denominational churches (Southern Baptist or Assembly of God) and independent congregations. These churches are often megachurches with names such as Church of the Open Door, Mariners Chapel, Community of Joy (in its blended/traditional services), Fellowship of Las Colinas, Willow Creek Community (on Wednesday and Thursday nights), and House of Hope. These full-service congregations and services are open and attractive.[8]

The audience for Praise and Worship is composed of both churched and unchurched believers. Most of the participants grew up in church, and often are the children of parents who attend Liturgical services. New members often come via transfer from Liturgical or other Praise and Worship congregations. These people know religious settings and traditional religious language, but feel more relaxed in an amphitheater, auditorium, cafeteria, or movie theater with a lectern. Without a visible communion table or baptismal font or pool, flexible seating allows each person to see the faces of others. Bulletins include announcements only and not an order of worship. The people participate in the service, most often through singing scriptural choruses and offering spontaneous prayers. Worship occurs on Sunday morning, Sunday night, or Wednesday night.

Because the Praise and Worship audience identifies more with brokenness and incomplete lives than with sin, the evangelistic task of the service is to be a therapeutic entry-way into the community of faith through justifying or converting grace. Whereas the Seeker service may be the steps and the Liturgical service the house, the Praise and Worship service is the front porch of the evangelistic task. The goal is to convince and teach young or less mature believers about God's love and God's will for their lives and then encourage them to continue their journey in the household of God. Rather than discovering God through art, gesture, signs, symbols, or tradition, this worship helps persons discover God within one's own self and immediate community. Baptism becomes the entryway into the community of faith, and Christian disciples are then formed in small groups led by mature believers. This approach reflects a more Aristotelian, as opposed to Platonic, way of knowing: people become not what they think but what they do. If persons do the right things in worship, these activities form them in the faith.

The shape of Praise and Worship is twofold: worship and teaching. Worship consists of singing some traditional but mostly contemporary music for an extended time, interspersed with extemporaneous prayers. Although no worship bulletin guides the congregation, leaders follow a developed pattern of worship and a rehearsed outline in each service. Singing lasts from fifteen minutes to an hour. Songbooks or overhead projection systems guide the singing, and the number of musicians and instruments varies. Teaching is the role of the teacher (not preacher), who most often interprets one extended passage of Scripture in an expository style. The sermon offers instruction and directions for Christian living, and extends from fifteen minutes to an hour. The personality and style of the teacher are critical. In general, these services are kerygmatic (proclamation of the Word) rather than eucharistic (sacramental) as is Liturgical worship.

Music is the most distinctive characteristic of Praise and Worship. The advent of new instruments, new tunes, and new texts has transformed the music found in these services. The songs are personal and corporate, enthusiastic and reflective, Christocentric and infused with the Holy Spirit. These choruses are often short (just one line or one verse) and usually taken directly out of Scripture (usually the King James Version). The music is syncopated, rather than having the straight beat of traditional hymnody, and often lacks four-part harmonies. Historically, this music fits within the musical tradition of African American spirituals, camp meeting choruses, nineteenth-century gospel hymnody, the venerable *Cokesbury Hymnal* (which was published fifty years ago for "young Christians"), youth retreats, campfire songs, and Hispanic corridos.[9] Much of this music comes out of theologically conservative traditions, and is promoted by a massive industry led by publishing and distributing giants such as Maranatha! Music and Integrity Music.

What is even more significant about the scriptural choruses is their function in worship. Classic hymnody focuses on strong, poetic texts about Scripture, set within the context of rich and complex music. The goal of these traditional hymns is to inform believers about the established faith and Scripture with which everyone is familiar. Moreover, believers are encouraged to use the texts and music of classic hymns for meditation and serious theological contemplation. Contemporary choruses, however, have no such interest. The goal instead is to create an environment of sound in which singers lose themselves. Functioning like an Eastern mantra, the ongoing repetition of scriptural texts and memorizable music transports singers from earth to heaven. The texts and music then begin to shape one's life. It is not unusual to sing a chorus at worship and then keep humming and singing that chorus for days.

One of the most exciting areas of Praise and Worship is the continuing creation of new Christian choruses. As more Liturgical congregations incorporate choruses into their worship, writers are increasingly composing choruses for Holy Communion, Baptism, and seasons of the Christian year. Generally, the songs are becoming more corporate and the language used of God and people is increasingly inclusive. The quality of the texts and tunes will probably improve in the coming decades.

The musician's title is worship leader, and the instrumentalists range from pianists to full house bands using guitars, drums, several keyboards, brass, and other instruments. The skill of musicians in the best of these services rivals that of night clubs, and the salary of the musician rivals that of the teacher. Digital electronic keyboards and percussion instruments abound. Digital hymnals (small music players containing thousands of songs and hymns) or computerized MIDI (musical instrument digital interface) systems occasionally replace all live musicians. Music may be accompanied by overhead projectors, slide projectors, synthesizers, video and data projectors, karaoke machines, and compact disc players with graphics display projectors.

Praise and Worship services introduced the church to new visual and aural technologies. Moving from overhead projectors to slide projectors and now to computer-generated video/data projection, everything in the worship service can be heard and seen: announcements, pictures of newborn babies, the scripture lessons, pictures and maps from the Holy Land, corporate prayers, recorded and real-time videos, and most commonly, songs. No longer does a new song have to be copyrighted and manufactured by a publishing house before congregations have access to it. The goal of the new technologies is to increase the participation of the congregation by involving more of their senses. The technologies encourage people to lift up their eyes and voices and free their hands.

Praise and Worship services also have critics, especially regarding music and theological content.[10] Although the tunes and texts of choruses stay in one's mind, like a radio jingle, the new music does not have the sophistication and integrity to last through the ages. Texts are still often predominantly filled with gender-exclusive language, both for persons and for God, with the primary image of God being the more archaic "Lord" (for which no contemporary Christian has any real reference—it brings to mind pictures of men who live in foreign countries, have lots of money, and dress extravagantly). Much of the language also focuses on personal experiences, emphasizing "my" relationship with God or how "I" praise God. In addition, a predominant use of contemporary music and choruses often closes the doors on classic and contemporary hymns. Critics in a similar fashion fault the message of these services. To churched believers, these Praise and Worship services appear superficial, simplistic, too accepting of contemporary culture, and lacking in substantive content; they merely create warm and fuzzy feelings with a focus on self-fulfillment. The emphasis on immediacy undercuts some essential aspects of worship such as the sacraments or a more holistic use of Scripture. Too rarely is Holy Communion celebrated or celebrated well, and the Old Testament is often neglected. As a sign of maturing, many of the Praise and Worship leaders are themselves asking, Is it a style in search of content?

Another major criticism of Praise and Worship concerns the role of their leaders. These services, according to their critics, appear to create personality cults centered on engaging teachers/preachers and worship leaders/musicians. Many folks ask, What will happen to these congregations when the founding pastor is no longer on the scene? In fairness, however, this question applies to autocratic leaders of any pattern of worship. There are a number of congregations of every kind built around the personality of a worship leader, all of which will have difficulty when the commanding pastor or musician leaves. The majority of Praise and Worship congregations, however, are not led by such personalities. In direct opposition, most of the successful congregations are nonhierarchical, having instead an effective leader who creates a worship team that uses many particular gifts to shape worship together. God has always used leaders, from Abraham to Moses to Miriam to Deborah to David. The major issue is how leaders will lead: either as autocrats who lead from personality or team leaders who shape a vision and share gifts. In general, Praise and Worship leaders appear willing and able to project a vision for worship and work with teams of worship leaders.

While many established worship leaders ask numerous questions about and often reject the Praise and Worship style, what cannot be denied is that significant numbers of North American Christians, especially younger generations and alienated Christians, are flocking to this style of worship. The children and grandchildren of churched believers from Liturgical churches are moving toward the Praise and Worship style.

Seeker Services

The third alternative in contemporary worship is a Seeker service. The original Seeker service is still found at the Willow Creek Community Church in a suburb of Chicago. Their Seeker services now occur four times on Saturday nights and Sunday mornings. This church meets on a large campus that resembles a mall more than a church. Parking lot attendants guide worshipers to parking spaces and a building with wide doors, without any evident Christian symbols. Information sheets, not worship bulletins, are distributed as thousands of people move into a high-tech auditorium. A professional ensemble warms up the audience with adult contemporary music. Then a drama team presents the issue of the day. The issues range from death to divorce to job changes to the birth of a child. Then the teacher appears and speaks about the issue raised. He suggests that Christ may have a solution to the problem of the day, and then invites the audience to come to the believers' worship service on Wednesday or Thursday night. An offering is taken, but visitors are encouraged not to sign, sing, or say anything unless they desire. Opportunities for small-group activities and interest groups are offered following worship. Approximately fifteen thousand people come to these weekend services. Worshiping communities around the United States, including Saddleback Valley Community Church in California and Community of Joy in Phoenix, now also offer Seeker services. Only a few established congregations, however, offer a true Seeker service.

These Seeker services are new and unique to our culture, and the most intriguing of the three options of contemporary worship. They offer Jesus to the unchurched or prechurched who did not grow up in church and are unfamiliar with traditional religious language or culture. The goal of Seeker services is not to gain new members on the church's roll but to introduce unbelievers to Jesus that they may have a vibrant relationship with Jesus. Other names for this group include "strangers to the gospel," "outsiders," "the marginalized," and "the overlooked." These seekers neither understand nor appreciate Liturgical or Praise and Worship services, which use predominantly traditional language and actions. The unchurched people want to worship anonymously and have the freedom not to participate. Many single adults and younger people are drawn to Seeker services, found normally in independent or radically creative congregations.

Places like the Crystal Cathedral in California, especially at its beginning, understand their ministry as one of outreach to the pre-Christian. Robert Schuller's approach is descriptive of their mission:

> the unchurched people's needs will determine our programs
> the unchurched people's hang-ups will determine our strategy
> the unchurched people's culture will determine our style
> the unchurched population will determine our growth goals.[11]

Seeker services are tightly choreographed presentations about contemporary real-life issues. Through word, sound, sight, and action, they present problems and offer solutions. The needs of seekers—to learn who God is, what the purpose of life is, how to forgive, how to deal with relationships, how materialism has failed, how to deal with suffering—are not unlike the needs of believers, but the presentation is radically different. A primary characteristic of these services is drama—through monologues, set skits, or improvisational theater—that asks seekers' questions as the prologue to a teacher's comments. While to an outsider the congregation appears passive, the services are intensely engaging. The teaching moves from the issues of a particular community of faith to scriptural texts.

All the Seeker services are informative, presenting Jesus to people who are perceived as neither sinful nor broken but ignorant. Leaders offer no pressure to join and simply invite people to enjoy the experience. Rob Frost, an evangelist of the British Methodist Church, is one proponent of this style. Frost ministers to seekers by offering improvisational theater skits in pubs and public venues of England and then invites persons to worship at local Methodist chapels. As Rick Warren, the senior pastor of Saddleback Valley Community Church, has written, "there are only three non-negotiable elements of a Seeker service: 1. treat unbelievers with love and respect; 2. relate the service to their needs; 3. share the message in a practical, understandable manner."[12] The evangelistic task of Seeker services provides the steps up to the porch and the church household, or, in traditional theological language, a precatechesis offering of prevenient grace. The goal is to introduce Jesus to people who know nothing about him.

The setting of Seeker services is more like a theater than church. There may be a stool and wireless microphone. An excellent video projection screen shows clips from television and movies. Persons sit in comfortable chairs or around round tables to facilitate conversation. No worship bulletins guide the services, which are more likely to be held on Friday or Saturday night or, for Willow Creek, on Sunday mornings. The services and every action within them assume no religious background whatsoever.

The shape of the service depends on the topic of the day. A lecture may follow a video, or a question-and-answer time may follow a song. Teaching tends to be thematic, explanatory, and didactic, with the pastor as a tour host leading a spiritual pilgrimage. The preaching pushes the borders of the kingdom of God out into the highways and byways. A worship team—including a speaker, band, band leader, lighting director, drama director/team, singers, choreographer, dancers—guides the worship. Many volunteers lead and support the service.

The music depends on the audience sought. Such services may use predominantly rock, jazz, rap, country, rhythm and blues, or folk music. Percussion instruments and tapes accompany the singing, most often sung only by soloists or choral group and not the congregation. Dress codes also vary dependent upon the dress of the desired audience: a speaker wearing cowboy boots leads a country service; a teacher wearing a button-down Oxford shirt and khaki pants speaks to baby boomers; a speaker with black jeans and a neon shirt addresses baby busters. There may or may not be a financial offering or an invitation to join the church community.

Seeker services come in two major styles: high participation or high performance. The high participation style, such as at Saddleback Valley Community Church, is a blended Seeker and Praise and Worship service. At Saddleback, unbelievers are invited to watch believers worship, and then join in when unbelievers feel comfortable. While the sermons are for seekers, the music includes both contemporary secular and sacred choruses, which the congregation joins in singing. The high performance style, such as at Willow Creek, uses contemporary secular and sacred music, drama, and basic Christian teaching. Here, the congregation may sing only one short chorus, greet one another briefly, and then be anonymous for the rest of the time.

Many observers wonder what eventually happens to seekers who participate in these services. Do they remain seekers all their lives or do they move to Praise and Worship and then Liturgical services? Typically, the effort is not to move seekers to Praise and Worship or Liturgical services, but to turn seekers into believers. While some seekers shift spiritual gears and move to other services, such a process is slow and uncertain. Willow Creek still has five times more seekers on Sunday morning than believers at its Praise and Worship on Wednesday and Thursday nights. Some mainline congregations near Willow Creek report some new members who transfer over from Willow Creek's Seeker services.

Most Seeker services understand church membership as driven by institutional needs (who will be sent offering envelopes), not the needs of seekers. Thus, most Seeker services downplay decisions "to join" the church. The more realistic and possibly faithful goal moves seekers from their services into small groups for Bible study and mission. The Seeker services by themselves do not create fully committed disciples of Jesus Christ; it takes more than one hour a week to create Christian disciples, and fundamentally these services do not invite such a response. Rather, congregations with Seeker services increasingly invite seekers to join small groups to deepen and enrich their faith, and in that setting invite persons into discipleship.

Problems also surround Seeker services. The lack of congregational participation appears to create personality cults built around the worship leaders. Many of these leaders, however, point to their work with worship teams as being collegial. Narrowly defined audiences, such as single professional baby boomers, often appear to exclude other people, although many such services appear to attract a wide ethnic diversity. Seeker services have the possibility of becoming a commodity or religious entertainment to be sold to specific audiences; success is measured in terms of market share. Technology, such as the latest computer graphics and projection, sometimes becomes an end unto itself. More substantially, only a few of those seekers who attend ever shift over to believers' services.

Most negatively, such worship sometimes appears to be "dumbing down" the faith to the lowest common denominator or to narcissistic personal needs. Many believers believe that true worship must necessarily consist of certain core beliefs and activities, and they resist any devaluing of these beliefs and activities. Supporters respond that the milk of the gospel is required before meat. In this light, most Seeker service leaders argue that their services are not really worship, but only an introduction to the faith that may invite persons into a fuller relationship with Jesus. For Seeker services to move persons into a fully committed relationship with Christ, there must be significant and intentional follow-up and teaching.

Liturgical, Praise and Worship, and Seeker services are all viable alternatives for the contemporary church. All three patterns of contemporary worship have theological integrity, yet each has significant problems. All three can be sensitive and adapt to surrounding culture. Even more so, all three also have the potential power to stand over and against any particular culture. Worship at its best is always acculturated—specific to a particular people, time, and place—and countercultural—a corrective to that particular culture. But where did these patterns originate? A review of recent liturgical reform and renewal will reveal their origins. Where contemporary worship has come from will tell much about where it is going, and how established congregations may respond.

2 | ORIGINS OF CONTEMPORARY WORSHIP

I f a faithful worshiping member of an established congregation fell asleep in the early 1960s and then awoke in
the late 1990s, the sleeper would be astounded at the
variety of worship options available. A whole new world of
worship has appeared. What happened?

What are the sources of contemporary worship? What are
the origins of Liturgical, Praise and Worship, and Seeker services? Out of what contexts have these liturgies arisen? The
simple answer is our recent culture. Fresh cultural realities,
new musical expressions, changing aesthetic values, and new
styles of personal expression demanded a fundamental
reevaluation of received worship traditions. In response,
denominational liturgical reforms of the late twentieth century and the advent of radically contrasting new styles of worship have sought to meet these modern realities. The responses from both within and beyond the established church
have led to contemporary worship in all its expressions.

Denominational Liturgical Reforms

What has happened in worship in The United Methodist
Church has parallels in every other old mainline denomi-

nation—Disciples of Christ, Episcopal, Lutheran, Presbyterian, Reformed, United Church of Canada, and United Church of Christ—in North America. The United Methodist Church, therefore, should serve to illustrate the changes that have occurred in the broader Christian tradition. In the 1980s and 1990s, The United Methodist Church sought to bring order to its worship life. In 1984, the United Methodist General Conference, the church's governing body, approved a convergence of worship resources in an effort to provide new authorized texts. It was hoped that these new texts would resolve a perceived liturgical uncertainty, even liturgical chaos. The forces unleashed in the movement toward convergence, however, sowed some of the very seeds of all the multiple options of worship now available.

The perception of chaos in the early 1980s arose out of a sense that the host of worship resources that had flooded the denomination had overwhelmed its worship leaders. These included the 1959 Evangelical United Brethren *Book of Ritual*, the 1965 Methodist *Book of Worship*, and seventeen volumes of the 1972–1985 Supplemental Worship Resource Series, along with official hymnals and unofficial songbooks. They were uneven, occasionally quixotic and idiosyncratic, and often theologically inconsistent. Generally, these liturgical resources, especially the earlier documents, reflected a hierarchical church dominated by men, focused on the needs of clergy and trained worship leaders, and leaned toward Anglican worship. Many of these resources appealed to Anglo United Methodists who wanted to be like low church Episcopalians.

These official United Methodist publications, however, did not include all the liturgical resources available. A multitude of independent and other denominations' material was also available and accessible to planners and leaders of worship. Major studies of Wesleyan liturgy and other liturgical traditions also appeared, prepared by a new generation of scholars. These young liturgists asked significant questions about present patterns of worship and offered distinctly new directions for the church at worship. By the mid-1980s, it took an entire bookshelf to contain a complete set of official and unofficial worship resources then available to church leaders and congregations. The time was ripe to restate the foundations of United Methodist worship and establish new patterns and styles of worship.

Beyond these liturgical pressures for change, many emerging cultural forces also demanded liturgical response. Clergywomen and laywomen, with their own unique theological and sociological insights, asked important questions about the theology, language, and hierarchical style reflected in worship. Society was increasingly becoming multicultural and global, and non-Anglo liturgists offered their own contributions to the worship arena. Western society was turning away from the printed word and bound texts toward an audio and video culture. Finally, generational gaps, especially among baby boomers, their parents, and the boomers' children and grandchildren demanded fundamental changes in worship.

The pressures for consolidation and cultural adaptation, along with a desire to express the gospel in fresh ways, led to the publication of the 1989 *United Methodist Hymnal* (primarily for congregations) and the 1992 *United Methodist Book of Worship* (primarily for planners and leaders of worship).[1] The 1992 General Conference adopted these two books as the only two English-language official worship resources of the denomination.[2]

These two resources are major contributions to United Methodist worship. These books serve clergy and laity (for instance, by using simpler rubrics to lead pastors and other worship leaders), align their contents with each other (e.g., cross-indexing), focus on Scripture (the lectionary becomes central), affirm racial and ethnic diversity (the inclusion of the Hispanic Advent/Christmas service of Las Posadas and a new appreciation for African American music, for example), reflect global diversity (illustrated by the prayer by the Sri Lankan D. T. Niles), acknowledge the increasing role and special needs of women in the church (as in the use of inclusive language and new lessons in the lectionary specifically dealing with women), recognize ecumenical liturgical reforms and convergence (e.g., the Word and Table pattern), and express a new appreciation for Wesleyan and evangelical traditions (like the Love Feast and the Invitation to Christian Discipleship). These two books are exceptionally comprehensive and set a high standard for prayerbooks and hymnals. Almost all United Methodist congregations currently use these two books, which are fundamentally shaping both the normative theology and practice of United Methodist worship.

Both *The United Methodist Hymnal* and *The United Methodist Book of Worship* possess a common set of worship assumptions. The first assumption is that worship patterns (in all their formal, printed manifestations) should be based on worship services from the first four centuries of the church (the patristic period of church history). A century-old effort at worship reform—in Roman Catholic reform movements culminating in Vatican II in the 1960s, and in Protestant worship renewal movements since the middle of this century leading to a new generation of hymnals and books of worship—has insisted that all Christian services be grounded in the services from the first centuries of the church.[3] The goal of these efforts was greater ecumenical unity: to discover ways in which diverse Christian communities could share common services of worship, by going back before the major church schisms. As a result, these early services provide the foundation of the United Methodist services for the Lord's Day and the sacraments. These same patristic-based services now parallel those services in almost all other recently published prayerbooks, signifying the triumph of the fourth century over the twentieth century in worship.

In addition to this emphasis on early church patterns, other worship assumptions controlled these two books. These included the perceived ability to blend evangelical and liturgical patterns of worship into a unified service (for example, adding an Invitation to Christian Discipleship as a Response to the Word), merge racial and cultural traditions (by including things like an African American Wake with the Services of Death and Resurrection), and combine a variety of hymnic musical styles (e.g., including non-Anglo hymns within classical Western hymnody). Also basic was a new appreciation for core Wesleyan liturgical understandings, such as the centrality of the preaching of the Word and a high view of the sacraments. The denomination adopted all of these assumptions, at least tacitly.

While there were a few major new efforts in these two official books, most notably the Daily Praise and Prayer services in the hymnal and the Healing services and Blessings for Persons in the book of worship, they were primarily conservative efforts of consolidation. The committees mainly used the printed resources of other churches in the classic Western liturgical tradition. The United Methodist committees, for example, conferred for the most part with Roman Catholics, Presbyterians, Episcopalians, and others in the broad Western liturgical tradition. These conversations enriched and enhanced established United Methodist worship in significant ways. The committees took what was available, used a common set of liturgical assumptions, and then created a rich collection of resources.

One fundamental problem, however, plagued *The United Methodist Hymnal* and *The United Methodist Book of Worship*: the people who developed these books. While this difficulty was recognized at the time both books were created, its major impact has become clear only in retrospect. This critique is not a personal attack on the skill and competence of the committees (on which this author sat), but an admission of who the committees were as compared with the rest of

North American society. While the committees were inclusive regionally, sexually, ethnically, and in other ways important to the denomination, in several critical ways they were very different from North American society. On the hymnal committee, five of the twenty-nine members were under forty years of age. All of the members had been raised in the church, believed in the essential integrity of the church's established worship, and were active participants in local congregations. On the book of worship committee, four of the twenty-two members were under forty, and all the members reflected the same value system and religious background as those on the hymnal committee. The committees compiled books of music and worship for themselves and for people just like them, lifelong believers who participated in established congregations each week.

Supportive of the work of the committees, almost all United Methodist and other academic liturgical scholars endorsed the conservative efforts. The scholastics supported revisions that offered an overwhelming concern for the past, endorsed past cultural and liturgical achievements, and used criteria for authentic worship that excluded creative new worship patterns that served distinctly different audiences. Thus, the books were created for people just like those who created them.

Advent of New Styles of Worship

At the same time committees in The United Methodist Church and in other communions such as the Presbyterian Church, U.S.A., the Christian Church (Disciples of Christ), The United Church of Canada, and the United Church of Christ were putting together new hymnals and books of worship, radically alternative congregations were developing within North America. Simultaneous with the official denominational efforts, alternative congregations with distinctly new worship patterns were developing and have now become a more visible and powerful force on the worship horizon.

The first set of these new congregations is entrepreneurial and noticeably nontraditional. Churches like Jubilee Community in Asheville, North Carolina, the Church of the Savior in Washington, D.C., Edgehill United Methodist in Nashville, Tennessee, and The Community in San Francisco, California—and noncongregational worship movements like the Woman Church movement—have pushed and continue to push worship in wholly unexpected ways. They each stretch worship to (or, some persons contend, beyond) the limits of Christianity. What is common to each of these congregations is that worship is the center of community life.

These congregations and movements discovered whole new audiences for worship. Many of the congregations exist in larger urban settings and attract audiences not served by any Christian church. The members tend to be single, younger, in alternative family units, and multicultural. Many people in each congregation have no church background, and bring a wide variety of spiritual backgrounds—from Zen Buddhism to African chants—to worship. The worship speaks to the needs of strangers seeking community. The liturgy is inventive, creative, and highly variable, and may reflect an evangelical Christian theology or a theology not recognizable as orthodox Christianity. The people worship in renovated homes, nightclubs, or cafeterias; the style is informal and the dress code highly relaxed. Charismatic leaders staff these congregations. Their music includes contemporary instruments such as synthesizers and unconventional instruments such as drums. The language tends to be inclusive, and ecological concerns are of high importance. These alternative congregations offer distinctly new ways of worshiping. Such models of worship still have not been taken seriously by worship leaders and professionals.

Congregations with a distinctive cultural tone (sometimes formed of new immigrants), a second source of new
worship patterns, have also arisen and stretch traditional
worship. African American congregations such as Imani
Temple in Washington, D.C., the African Roman Catholic
Church in Chicago, or Ben Hill United Methodist Church in
Atlanta present worship that is unashamedly black and
beautiful. The dress, music, rituals, and preaching are first
and foremost targeted to modern, urban African Americans. Likewise, Korean, Native American, Hispanic, South
Asian, and Hmong congregations (all of which have many
variations and subsets of communities), among many others, are also creating new worship styles that reflect and
address predominantly one cultural community. Especially
among new immigrant populations in the United States,
worship is recognizably different from that found in established congregations. In The United Methodist Church over
the past decade, new songbooks and hymnals, with liturgies and songs radically unlike any seen before, have
appeared for each of the above named nonmajority
racial/ethnic communities. Worship fragmentation along
ethnic and cultural lines is increasing. No one hymnal or
book of worship of any tradition will ever again be able to
encompass the wholeness of all racial/ethnic expressions of
worship.

Finally, there are the neo-evangelical, sometimes neo-
pentecostal, churches arising in urban centers and in many
small towns and communities. Often led by young believers who did not have a churched background, these
congregations reach out to persons for whom established
worship does not speak, or more significantly who have
never before been in any church. Some of these congregations are megachurches, but most of these churches remain
quite small. Sometimes related to the church growth movement, their style of worship has been categorized as "effervescent," filled with spirited singing and engagement of

the emotions.[4] They are modern heirs of the pietistic (stressing personal holiness) movements of the eighteenth century among Lutheran, Reform, and Methodist traditions and the revivalistic camp meetings on the American frontier in the nineteenth century. Charles G. Finney, who described and systematized this revivalistic pattern in his famous 1837 *Lectures on the Revivals of Religion*, wrote that the emphasis in these congregations should be on immediate human experience.[5] The experience of the Brownsville Assembly of God in Pensacola, Florida, which has a several-year revival in process, is one such expression of this worship style.

Nevertheless, in spite of all these developments, the hymnal and book of worship committees of every mainline church had too little conversation with any of these alternative congregations. For example, churches and their worship leaders who did not have a prayerbook tradition were not invited to contribute. Many of these nonliturgical churches have a rich tradition of different styles of worship and are experimenting with new ones. The committees did not seriously investigate the contributions of these other worshiping communities of faith whether radically new, distinctly cultural, or neoevangelical. The debate about hymns, for example, consisted of how many ethnic hymns versus old gospel choruses versus classic hymns versus new hymns would be included; contemporary evangelical Christian choruses or Hispanic corridos did not receive adequate attention.

In summary, the field of vision of the formal hymnal and book of worship committees was too narrow, and the books created were for believers whose sensitivities were like those of the believers who sat on the committees. When placed in a growing secular culture in which radically new patterns and styles of worship were emerging, the official resources reflected too narrow a perspective.

New Horizons

An image for visualizing this process is a high mountain pass. Imagine a mountain range with only one narrow gap for passage through the mountains. After a long and tortuous journey upward, a pilgrim arrives at the top of the range and stands before the pass. Much time, energy, money, and expertise have been spent to make the journey thus far. The journey, seemingly, has been successful. But then, when the pilgrim moves through the narrow gorge, a startling vista surprises the pilgrim. A whole new land, unimagined, stands before the sojourner. The pilgrim now realizes that the journey has just begun.

The United Methodist worship reforms of 1984 to 1992, like those reforms in every establishment denomination, took the vast array of worship resources then available, worked diligently with these resources, narrowed them down, and focused them into official books. Much of the winnowing and refocusing added value to Liturgical worship. The goal, seemingly, was the creation of definitive new books of worship. But then, just as the denominations published new books, a whole new world appeared.

This journey toward new hymnals and books of worship opened Pandora's box. By listening to voices asking for change and being responsive to different communities, the reform of worship patterns and styles could no longer look just to the past or to believers' voices or seek to be responsive only to professional liturgists. As James White has observed, "centralized ecclesiastical control of worship" may inhibit liturgical reform, but it always fails to stop it completely.[6]

At present, what is happening is that new cultures are opening radically new horizons. The past alone cannot solely prepare for the future. New Christian voices offer unconventional possibilities unimagined by any centralized or commanding authority. Authentic communication of the gospel demands new styles. The journey toward God through authentic worship continues.

3 GENERATIONAL CULTURE WARS

What new world must contemporary worship serve? Present North American culture is vastly different from the society of only a decade ago. New communities, new ways of communicating, and new opportunities stand before the church.

Many established Christian congregations parallel the following history: First Church began as a neighborhood congregation. Built one hundred years ago in a small village, First Church was established by families who worked in town. A few members still remember the early decades. The church grew slowly, just as the town grew slowly. The church hit its peak in the 1950s when new babies and children filled the church. After the 1950s, however, the congregation's membership became older as children and grandchildren of the church grew up and moved away. The neighborhood changed. Young families, unrelated to the older members, moved into the community. Some of these new families drive ten miles away to a larger, full-service congregation, but most adults born since 1945 and their families stay at home on Sunday mornings. Now, primarily older adults worship at First Church. Only a few members are under fifty-five years of age, and each of them grew up in a church home. Worship attendance drops every year.

Among the cultural changes affecting every local congregation, generational differences have had the most significant impact on worship. The builder generations (born before 1945), the baby boomers (born from 1945 to 1964), the baby busters (born from 1965 to 1976), and the millennials (born since 1976) are radically different from one another. The following stereotypes of these generations, while imperfect, nevertheless help describe the worlds these generations inhabit and the impact of these generations on worship.

Builder Generations (born before 1945)

The builder generations are composed of two groups, the GI generation (born from 1908 to 1926) and the silent generation (born from 1927 to 1944). Today they are over fifty-five years old. Growing up and forming a culture characterized by material restriction, frugality, loyalty, and self-denial, these generations were raised in small towns and rural settings and were shaped by the Great Depression and the two World Wars. They created a strong United States and swore that their children would benefit from all they could provide. Their heroes included Charles Lindbergh and Amelia Earhart. Lyndon Johnson and Ronald Reagan were members of this generation who became President. Big bands ruled the new radio airways, and organs dominated church music. The builders believe that the United States is a Christian country, and an overwhelming number accept that belonging to a local congregation is valuable. Family and social roles are rigid and personal, while individual expectations are high. Established value systems are affirmed and rarely questioned. While these builder generations are one-fourth (approximately sixty-eight million people) of the United States population, in The United Methodist Church these generations constitute almost two-thirds of the members and over half of those who participate in worship.

Theologically, these builder generations affirm an ethic of self-denial. They emphasize the family, church, and nation as predominant over the individual; the community is more important than the self. They see God as Judge and Ruler, transcendent in the heavens. Creation exists for the benefit of human beings. Sinful people have rejected God, but Christ's atonement on the cross saves people from their sin. Scripture is the ultimate law book, and the church offers refuge from a sinful world. Builders defined and still control most established congregations. Moreover, these people shaped and still appreciate much of Liturgical worship, against which many of their children and grandchildren are now rebelling.

The builder generations are currently undergoing significant change. As their families have grown and moved away, so their own needs and relationship to the church change. Retirement, for example, opens the possibility for frequent travel or even moving to a whole new community. Empty nests and retirement years sometimes lead to increasing marriage difficulties; financial freedom offers whole new opportunities for growth; but financial anxiety leads to less generosity. The impact of these changes on the church is just beginning. For example, some congregations have discovered increasing numbers of older adults who no longer attend worship or give regularly. Some of the builder generations are vocal when a congregation targets younger generations. The majority of established congregations are still controlled by builders, who thus control a congregation's worship. The builders still need much ministry and care, and they ask the church how they will continue to be served.

Baby Boomers (born from 1945 to 1964)

Baby boomers, children of the builder generations, are the single largest segment (seventy-eight million people, almost one-third of our population) of North American culture. These boomers have affected every aspect of our culture. Growing up during the era of the Civil Rights movement and the Vietnam War, the freedom of the 1970s, and the Reagan boom years shaped a generation of free spirits. Their heroes included Martin Luther King, Jr., John F. Kennedy, and Gloria Steinem. They grew up with rock and roll (today's Oldies) and the Mickey Mouse Club. They yearn to be proactive change-agents who will create a just and humane society. Urban dwellers, they live alone or in smaller, blended families with both partners working.

These boomers are consumers who want to be served and expect to make choices—short-term, concrete, and immediate—in every aspect of life. They desire high quality and instant gratification from food to sex to faith. Often greedy, materialistic, and narcissistic, they seek intimacy and authenticity, yet find it difficult to offer or accept such closeness. Their search for new experiences drives them to constant change. Boomers are innovative yet pragmatic, work-driven yet desiring personal space. Viewing all truth as relative, they are asking questions and wanting answers. They are secular, the majority did not grow up in church, and, in their own view, are nonracist and tolerant. They are the last generation of the Enlightenment and thus are persons who believe that the world can be explained in scientific and rational ways. They are biblically and musically illiterate; television and radio inform and set norms for behavior. But as the boomers move into middle age, they are desperately searching for meaning, values, and truth. As Craig Miller has described them, they are broken, lonely, without roots, and searching for truth.[1]

One of the difficulties in dealing with baby boomers is their diversity. Some of the boomers are very conservative and traditional, while others are exceptionally liberal and innovative, and the majority fall somewhere in between. Bill Clinton and Rush Limbaugh in their values and failures represent both the commonalities and the diversity of these thirty- and forty- and early fifty-somethings. Other categories of boomers include everything from yuppies (young urban professionals) to hardworking people at the margin of economic success. Of course, every classification has major exceptions.

The theology of the boomers, however, is consistently one of self-fulfillment—almost the polar opposite of their parents' generation. In their search for meaning, they have tried Eastern gurus and self-actualization seminars. Delving into New Age faiths, they have read *The Celestine Prophecy* and they watch for angels. Joseph Campbell's mythic hero describes their journey of faith. The ethic of self-fulfillment has now become a dominant perspective shared by many folks in all living generations. Builders who drive expensive mobile homes displaying the bumper sticker "I'm driving my child's inheritance" demonstrate its pervasiveness.

For the boomers, God is the benevolent creator of the universe, present in all things, and always accessible. God made all creation and all people good in God's own image. Alienation from God is not thought of as sin but as incompleteness and emptiness. Jesus personifies a good teacher to whom people should listen. Scripture provides a road map, and the church is one of many locations for discovering God. Less than half of this generation believes that belonging to a church is valuable. While some boomers have always been and always will be churched believers, others have never been in a sanctuary and show no interest in church, and still others do not know what to believe. These boomers want leaders who will show them how life works, using whatever religious or other authorities are available. Boomers who grew up in Liturgical worship are increasingly attracted to Praise and Worship, while their unchurched contemporaries are discovering Seeker services.

Busters and Millennials (born since 1965)

Finally, the next generations will increasingly define North American culture and shape the worship of all congregations.[2] The baby busters or generation X or the thirteenth generation, the youngest siblings or children of the boomers, are the second most powerful generation affecting our culture. Almost forty-five million (15 percent of the U.S. population) of these twenty-somethings live in an electronic and computer culture grounded in a fast, oral, sound-bite age, shaped from childhood by *Sesame Street*. They watch and listen to music, from rock to rap to country, on MTV, VH1, and CMT. They are the first postmodern generation which no longer believes in strictly scientific and materialistic descriptions of the world. Stressed out, disillusioned, and alienated, they are searching for families they never had. Born in an age with the pill and abortion, their parents told them that they are a wanted generation. Yet they feel neglected and ignored by the self-denial builders and the self-fulfillment boomers. Busters come from broken homes, missing parents, and declining schools; they are the original daycare and latchkey kids. They saw the marriage and divorce of Prince Charles and Lady Diana, Lady Diana's search for independence and her death, space travel and the *Challenger* explosion, and the deterioration of the environment in the midst of Earth Days.

Committed to personal activism and issues such as saving whales or rain forests, the baby busters invented cyberspace and cruise the Internet. Fear of AIDS defines their curious, casual, and cautious sex life. Pessimistic about the future, the busters feel lost and alone, and lack hope financially, vocationally, relationally, and spiritually. Unlike the boomers, who live to work, this generation works to live. They are becoming deeply competitive and believe that their own individual hard work will grant success. Skinheads are the anarchists of the busters; Kurt Cobain's suicide makes sense to them; *Friends* and *Seinfeld* are their television shows. Unlike their parents' and grandparents' ethics—self-denial or self-fulfillment—their ethic is survival. The baby busters do not comprehend self-denial and feel abused by self-fulfillment.

Their ethic of survival has distinctive contours. The busters are uncertain if there is a God, are ignorant of Jesus Christ and the Bible, and consider the church irrelevant. God is a vague spirit somewhere else, Jesus is an ancient teacher, and heaven and hell are mythic constructs. As the first generation to have grown up in a wholly secular public school system, they recognize no moral or religious absolutes other than "what works." The only absolute is situation ethics. They are radically independent; all corporate institutions are suspect. A majority of the busters are unchurched, and only one-third believe belonging to local congregations is valuable.

Despite their distance from the church, the busters are seeking an environment led by caring healers or mentors who accept them as they are, foster deep relationships, focus on their real-life issues, and offer them hope. Feeling like outsiders, they want to be inside a community that is greater than the individual. The worship they desire is low-tech (helps them slow down) and high-touch (fosters deep relationships), with sermons that do not so much offer answers as identify and name their own unique questions. The primary media to reach the busters include their own music, multisensory presentations, and personal stories that connect them to others. Jesus' humanity, compassion, and faithfulness to himself and his friends speaks to this generation. Oprah Winfrey's conversational style of identifying questions and offering possible solutions works well with the busters. A majority describe themselves as religious, even Christian.

Finally, there is the emerging generation, the millennials, also named blasters or generation Y. These millennials are under twenty-three years old (born since 1976), the generation born to the late-childbearing boomers (two-thirds of them) and early-childbearing busters. These millennials are second only to the baby boomers in number (seventy-two million or 27 percent of the U.S. population). One-third of them have been born out of wedlock, and some commentators suggest that there will be a class war between the haves (who live in two-income homes) and the have-nots (who live in single-parent/income homes). Half of this generation already lives in blended homes or with just one parent. They listen to grunge rock, rap, and country music. Trained to work in teams, they are not yet sure of the role of the individual.

Too much is still uncertain about the millennials, but what is clear is that what worked for the preceding generations does not work for them. This generation initially appears to be focused on the outer world of science, math, economics, and politics, not the inner world of their emotions. They seem more self-confident, less worried about nuclear destruction, more supportive of independent political parties, environmentally astute, egalitarian, and less concerned about making money. Their worries include AIDS, pollution, street violence, and terrorism. Like previous generations, they remain distrustful of government, health systems, the media, and the church. Hooked to the Internet and not network television, they will be radically independent. While the millennials' religious views are still in flux, the church is just one of many ways to discover God and has no place of prominence in their lives. Unfortunately, very few in this generation appear attracted to worship of any kind. Locations such as military bases, where there are high concentrations of busters, may offer the best models of worship for this generation and its successor, the millennials. Military chaplains, who focus by necessity on people of this age range, may possess the worship tools to reach these generations.

Millennials, even those born and raised in the homes of believers, are clearly the most neglected group of seekers. Remembering that Christians are not born but made, each congregation must ask itself whether its own children and the unchurched friends of its children are learning anything about the essentials of Christian faith and life. Is a congregation's worship and Christian formation creating a generation that will continue the gospel? For this generation, the Roman Catholic model of systematic Christian formation through liturgy and teaching, now being imitated by Episcopalians, Lutherans, and most recently United Methodists, is one response. Every congregation that wishes to serve seekers must have at least some focus on children and youth.

In short, the builders, boomers, busters, and millennials are radically different cultures coinhabiting North American society. Their backgrounds, worldviews, and experiences are all radically different from one another. One final way to describe their differences is to mention how the young men of each generation approached international armed conflict. In World War II, many young men of the builder generation left jobs, communities, wives, and children to volunteer to fight overseas. Very few builders questioned the value of denying self and family, even to death, to defend one's country and ideals. During the Vietnam War, many boomers did everything necessary to resist or dodge the draft; their cry was "Hell no, we won't go." During the Gulf War, one of the busters going into battle was quoted: "Why am I fighting this war declared by an older generation? Get me out of here alive." Finally, the millennials have no shared memory of any international conflict at all. Unfortunately, most established congregations are trying to serve all of these different generational cultures with one homogeneous pattern and style of worship.

Impact on Worship

The impact of the new generations, especially the boomers and busters, upon the North American religious world is dramatic. Currently, there are over two thousand active religious faiths in the United States. The old categories—Protestant, Jewish, and Catholic—are outdated. In addition to members of other religious groups, many people are simply secular, with almost two-thirds of our society unchurched. While worship attendance in established congregations drops every year, new evangelical churches often supplant the old mainline churches as the churches of choice for those who go to worship, yet all these churches together serve an increasingly smaller proportion of the total population. Charismatics, Jesus People, and nondenominationalists are now respected members of the community, yet too often speak a religious language that many in the culture cannot interpret. Denominational loyalty does not exist, and church-hopping and selective participation in church activities dominate. The new generations, however, still express deep spiritual thirst. Seeking community and direction, small groups and twelve-step communities for growth, recovery, and companions on the spiritual journey spring forth everywhere.

Many established Christian believers condemn these new secularized generations and criticize their lack of loyalty to the church. The old establishment loyalists yearn for the new generations to repent and return to the established church and its worship. Parents and grandparents wait for their children and grandchildren to grow up and come back to church. Older folks still expect the new generations to turn off their rock and roll radio stations and buy season tickets to the symphony. When the new generations stay away, the establishment condemns them loudly. A bishop, preaching at an annual gathering of clergy, once condemned the new generations who come to worship and ask how a congregation can meet their needs. When the bishop proclaimed: "The question is not how the church can serve you, but how you can serve the church," he received a standing ovation. The believers inside the church were again criticizing the seekers outside the church for not being like believers. The problem, however, is not how the outsiders see the church, but how the church sees the outsiders.

Many Christians see this age as a time of great opportunity. George Hunter, for example, suggests that in this secular, postmodern world, hundreds of millions of people are ready to hear the Christian gospel; there remains a window of opportunity. The story, however, must be told in new ways.[3] Fortunately for both these new generations and the church, even while the older generations control the purse strings and decision making in established churches, many boomers, busters, and possibly millennials are willing to give the church one more try or try it for the first time. When they do, the primary entry point is worship.

Worship is the key to reaching the newer generations. Seekers or pre-Christians come first to corporate worship to see if the church has something to offer. What the younger generations often do not want and cannot relate to in worship is what they saw, heard, and experienced in childhood. What they remember is negative: boring sermons, slow music, clerical domination, stained-glass windows, hard pews, racial segregation, long anthems in Latin, people dressing up, verbose prayers, a cold atmosphere, institutional self-concern (always asking for money), and no one who looks like them. Congregations too often appear as strange, unfriendly, and irrelevant. Rather, these new generations are looking for worship that is expressive, interactive, open to a variety of family models, willing to help shape values, and accepting of informal dress. They welcome culturally and racially inclusive congregations in which women are respected and everyone participates at whatever level he or she desires.

Other observers of our culture and worship have interpreted the impact of the newer generations on worship in similar ways. Robert Webber, a liturgist who commends

Liturgical worship to Praise and Worship leaders, believes that many in the new generations seek worship in which stark rationality is replaced by mystery, observation by experience, logic by paradox, transcendence by immanence, the head by the heart, information by formation, silence by sound, individuality by community, and isolation by touch. The new generations ask, "Have I experienced God in this place?" The reasonable, logical, informational worship of the older generations has been rejected.[4]

Wade Clark Roof, a church sociologist, has defined the impact on worship in similar ways. Roof sees a desire for subjective experiences in which persons come to church for high-tech services that promise intimacy and healing. No longer trusting the foundations of Western liturgy or religious authorities, these new generations desire large group celebrations and small group experiences, each of which must exhibit a spontaneous character filled with sound and a focus on personal growth.[5]

Tim Wright, a nontraditional Lutheran pastor at the Community of Joy in Phoenix, believes that contemporary persons, and especially boomers, come to churches that offer a safe environment, focus on people's needs, offer choices including teaching ministries, promote a vision for the future, and worship through excellent messages and music.[6]

America's most prominent church historian, Martin Marty, describes the most alive churches today as those which praise God, welcome the stranger, inventory actual needs in their communities, and heal.[7] For congregations, however, that do not serve the new generations and for the new generations themselves, the future is bleak. Gregor Goethals, as quoted in *Christian Worship and Technological Change*, declares, "Until institutional religion can excite . . . the soul and evoke the fullness of human passion, television will nurture our illusions of heroism and self-transcendence."[8]

Clearly the new generations expect worship that is quite different from that of their parents and grandparents. The landscape of new worship is definitely a new environment. A strange new world has now emerged. Radically different generations live together, but disjointedly; attempt to understand one another but speak different languages; and worship together with a great diversity of expectations. Parents, children, and grandchildren all inhabit the same complex world and live in crisscrossing arenas including worship. While the church must honor the past and those who have been and continue to be shaped by the past, nevertheless, Christians at worship must also honor the present and future and serve the new generations and their needs and expectations. The church, as always, is only one generation away from extinction. Liturgical change is necessary if the church's children and grandchildren and their unchurched friends are to have faith.

In the second chapter of Acts, on the Day of Pentecost, persons from every point of the earth heard the good news in their own languages. The Holy Spirit did not insist that all of them hear in one language only. Rather, the Word spoke directly to persons from very different cultures in their own tongues. The task currently before the church is to speak directly to the multiple cultures in our society in their own languages. Missionaries who serve in foreign lands first learn the native language and try to understand the culture before they proclaim the gospel. In North American culture, those who plan and lead worship must also learn new languages and become aware of different cultures (particularly the generational cultures), if they wish to proclaim the gospel clearly.

As congregations evaluate their own style of worship, consider alternative patterns of worship, and blend elements of one pattern with another, however, the fundamental question arises again: What is the purpose of worship?

4 WORSHIP AS A MEANS OF GRACE

In 1919, a committee of the Methodist Episcopal Church declared that a painting at Central Methodist Episcopal Church in Columbus, Ohio was "the best known picture in America." The painting—*The Wyandot Indian Mission*—depicts the first mission of the Methodist Episcopal Church at Upper Sandusky, Ohio.

A dramatic story stands behind the painting. John Stewart, an African American freeman, had lived "a drunken and dissolute life." In early 1816, Stewart was on his way to a river to end "his worthless existence, until attracted by a worship service in a Methodist congregation he was passing." Stewart "heard the singing, hesitated, entered the church, and was gloriously converted." Following his conversion, Stewart felt a strong call to go and preach the gospel of Jesus Christ to the Wyandot Indians. By November 1816, he had established a mission among the Wyandot Indians by preaching the gospel in the Wyandot language. He inspired the organization of the Parent Mission Board of the Methodist Episcopal Church in New York in 1819. When Stewart died in 1823, J. B. Finley, an Anglo circuit rider, continued this native-language ministry to the Wyandots.

The painting commemorates this story. A one-room, gray-stone sanctuary—one door for men and another door for women—stands in the background of the painting. A multi-ethnic gathering of people fills the foreground. Stewart wears the rough clothing of a freeman, with his long hair bound in Wyandot fashion. Finley wears the black clothing of a circuit rider. Some forty Wyandot men, women, and children in native clothing encircle the church. No copy of a Methodist hymnal or other worship resource is visible. Stewart had a passion for unchurched Native Americans; therefore he used their language and wore his hair like the Indians to communicate the gospel. His efforts led to the formal organization of missionary efforts of the Methodists.[1]

Why worship? Why is it important? What is the purpose of worship? The answers to these questions are fundamental in any discussion of worship in any place and time. The debate over the nature and purpose of worship, which has been going on since the creation of the church, still rages today. Even more critical, different theological answers to these questions have a profound impact on worship patterns. It is now time to engage in some God-talk (theology) and understand the implications of various theological positions on the practice of worship in local congregations.

In the Wesleyan theological tradition, worship is a means of grace; worship expresses God's reality and presence in ways through which people can both hear and respond to the gospel. The issue for Wesleyans is not whether a particular worship service is textually correct or historically accurate or rubrically appropriate, but whether worship effectively communicates the saving story of God's mighty acts to a particular people. The goal for every worship service is to effect a new relationship between God and each individual present. Faithful to this Wesleyan tradition, John Stewart shared the good news with the Wyandots, not through John Wesley's *Sunday Service of the Methodists in North America* of 1784 or the liturgies found in the Methodist *Disciplines* of his age, but through worship uniquely adapted to a wholly new people.[2] We face the same challenge.

Wesley's Means of Grace

In his landmark sermon "The Means of Grace," John Wesley describes the scriptural and ordinary channels wherein God conveys to everyone the prevenient, justifying, and sanctifying grace that they need.[3] According to Wesley, through the communal means of grace—the Word of God, the sacraments of Baptism and Holy Communion, corporate prayer, and Christian community—persons receive God's grace.

Wesley specifically mentions several forms of grace. Prevenient grace (grace that goes before, like preventive medicine) affirms God's presence. This presence convicts people of their sin and enables persons to respond to God's initial call. Justifying grace reestablishes a positive relationship, making persons daughters and sons of the Almighty. Sanctifying grace leads people to fullness of relationship, that is, to a life lived in perfect harmony with God. As Wesley declared, "There is but one scriptural way wherein we receive inward grace—through the outward means [acts of worship] which God hath appointed."[4]

Through the Word of God read, proclaimed, and responded to, the sacraments of Baptism and Holy Communion rightly offered and received, community prayer lifted and heard, and gathering for fellowship in community, God offers salvation and calls persons to faithful discipleship. While Wesley admits that it is possible for God to offer grace in extraordinary ways not dependent upon these corporate worship experiences, he declares that he never witnessed such an act of grace. While God may make disciples as they sit alone on top of a mountain or as they walk along a beach, such actions at best are not the norm and at worst undercut the scripturally described ways through which God saves. Wary of a too-Protestant emphasis on personal faith or a too-Catholic emphasis on sacramental efficacy, Wesley emphasizes both God's actions and human response in worship. Wesley claims that worship, in which God's gift of grace unites with individual faith through the ordinary established patterns of the church, is the primary means through which God offers salvation. Worship is drawn forth by God and transforms human lives. As described by Adrian Burdon, "the purpose of worship, here being stated by Wesley, is the bringing of the people to resemble the God whom they worship."[5]

Wesley's liturgical approach holds both gospel and human experience in tension. On the one hand, Wesley faithfully holds to the substance of received orthodox and classical Christianity. On the other hand, Wesley is remarkably sensible of and sensitive to the situation of those whom he taught and to whom he preached. Wesley's questions are: What must people hear and how are they able to hear? In answering the first, Wesley returns to traditional theology, especially in his concern for human salvation. In answering the second question, he possesses remarkable awareness of the intellectual, social, and moral ethos in which people live. Wesley's astounding success is due to the holism he achieves in his sensitivity to both dimensions.

This practical use of worship parallels Wesley's unique theological method. For Wesley, theology is not so much for the purpose of understanding life or abstractly defining God; rather theology is intended to change lives. Theology's purpose is to underwrite the preaching and service of the gospel. Wesley's theology has been accurately described as "practical divinity."[6] This practical theology brings the gospel and life together, making clear the message of God's grace for structuring gracious Christian living.

The implications of Wesley's theological approach are profound for worship. In preaching, for example, the polar dynamic between preacher and hearer; between essential message and existential human reality; between what should be said and what can be heard; between the gospel that transforms life and lives that can be vitalized by the gospel is impossible to separate. Preached and received Word are so tightly intertwined that they cannot be pulled apart without damage to both. Preaching is intended to evoke response; the gospel is proclaimed in order to transform life. While the message to be proclaimed is foundational, likewise the context in which the message is proclaimed must be understood equally with due sensitivity and adroit interpretation.

Wesley's theological method and its resulting vision of worship had profound implications for the eighteenth-century Wesleyan revival. Because of his passion to proclaim God's grace in ways that people in his culture, shaped by the Enlightenment and Industrial Revolution, could understand and to which they could respond for the sake of salvation, Wesley initiated a liturgical revolution. He became a traveling evangelist and used nonlectionary texts chosen for particular audiences and settings. He preached outdoors on Hanham Mount, at the gates of coal mines, and in an abandoned arms factory. Wesley celebrated the sacraments outdoors and encouraged extemporaneous prayer. The Love Feast, a time of holy sharing adapted from the German Moravians, became a popular Wesleyan celebration. Charles Wesley wrote hymns based not on a metrical psalter but on religious poetry, and set these hymns to existing, sometimes popular, tunes, which was as offensive to his religious culture as it is offensive to established congregations to sing "Amazing Grace" to the tune of "Gilligan's Island." The Wesleys encouraged women to sing and laypeople to speak in church. In North America, Methodist circuit riders were appointed not to established congregations but to vast regions to establish missions, with liturgies unique to the North American setting. In summary, because of the Wesleyan perspective that worship exists for the sake of the spiritual transformation of persons through the power of the gospel, the Wesleys and their heirs broke many established liturgical traditions.[7]

Opponents to Wesley

This Wesleyan liturgical perspective, however, has its opponents. Critics who object to adapting worship to a particular culture or community argue that such adaptations ignore that God is the primary audience in worship. Some persons believe that either holding tight the tension between honoring God and recognizing human need or, what is worse, beginning with people and their needs fundamentally denies the central focus of worship: honoring God. Søren Kierkegaard, a nineteenth-century Danish theologian, best described this theological position when he declared that God is the audience of worship and members of the congregation are the players on the stage. Today, many theologians and professional liturgists reject any adaptations to worship because the needs of people must be kept secondary to the worship of God.

The classic position of Wesley's critics is rooted in the Reformed tradition (following John Calvin). For Reformed theologians, as expressed by the Council of Dort of 1619, as well as in the majority theological position of the Church of England, worship is primarily for the glorification of God. The Westminster Catechism, an Anglican collection of theological questions and answers, reflects this tradition as it begins: "What is the chief end of humans? A human being's chief end is to glorify God, and to enjoy God forever." Reformed theology stresses giving God praise and honor. Worship is primarily directed to God, and a community is gathered primarily to honor God. This theological tradition is shared today in essential thrust by Roman Catholics, traditional Baptists, Presbyterians, and Lutherans, along with the great majority of professional liturgists and many Methodists. This God-centered theological perspective is often the primary argument for why worship must not change to suit people. Attention must be given to God whether or not persons hear the gospel in transforming ways.

The clear alternative to John Calvin was the Dutch theologian Jacobus Arminius, through his *Remonstrance* of 1610 and one of his spiritual heirs, John Wesley. In the Arminian theological tradition, God has intervened in all human lives with prevenient grace, a grace offered to every person prior to and as the basis of any human response. Persons, who by nature are sinful, are not left to themselves; God is always working with people toward the end that all might have the possibility of being saved. By grace, human beings are gifted with response-ability, with the freedom of will to choose or reject God's love. Salvation is an interaction of God's initiative and human response.

Arminian liturgy is not only for the purpose of praising and enjoying God. It expands that vision to include the goal of offering Christ for human acceptance. God's action is gratefully acknowledged and persons are encouraged to respond. An Arminian understanding of "glory" means allowing the light of God to show through those who worship. There is a convergence of emphasis: the worship of God represents acceptance of grace, gratitude expressed to God, and our committed participation in the event. One implication of this perspective has to do with preaching. Preaching in the context of worship must present God's grace in Jesus Christ, evoke response, and encourage people to work out their own salvation; worship experiences such as hymn-singing or prayer or the sacraments are also occasions for transforming life.[8]

Implications

The challenge today for Christian congregations is to find a holistic interaction of presentation and reception, of the enduring message of the gospel linked with a changing culture. To present the Christian gospel meaningfully, the message must be set in the actual context of present life. The message and the media must both be relevant to establish a vital relation between God and persons; vitality and integrity can be joined. Contexts change and so does relevancy. Every new generation needs new voices and fresh retelling of God's story. Only through relevant clarity are people able to hear and respond. The challenge for worship is to remember clearly God's grace and to tell the good news in contemporary language that is sensitive to changing cultural contexts.

Paul, in 1 Corinthians 9, helps establish this balance. Speaking to the Gentile culture, radically unlike his own Jewish culture, Paul argues that gospel and culture are dynamically related. Culture is a vehicle to convey the gospel, but culture is not the gospel. Accommodation is necessary, but conformity is not. The line between gospel and culture is thin; dangers are rife. Becoming all things to all people, however, is necessary in order that the gospel may be adequately and effectively conveyed. To put it simply, Paul proclaimed the same gospel that Peter did, but he had to do so in new ways.

New presentations of the gospel have always enriched the church. Innovations in worship have been made throughout the ages in response to changing cultures. Effective worship through the centuries demonstrates that sensitivity to God and to changing human situations is re-creative. In all ages, the church at its best has understood the need to express the gospel in ways that each particular culture or new generation may understand. New forms of worship have always arisen within the great revivals of the church. Shaping worship to speak an authentic gospel to a particular cultural context is the Christian tradition! Worship serves a living God and living peoples.

Despite some pleas to the contrary, the Bible has never dictated only one way to worship. The Incarnation—God taking human form—witnesses to God's affirmation of humanity in a particular cultural context. Jesus, the Word become flesh, preached inside and outside of the synagogue and temple and took the gospel to a lake, mountainsides, homes, and streets. Peter invited Gentiles into the church, and Philip witnessed in a chariot to an Ethiopian eunuch. At the first Jerusalem Conference (as found in the Acts of the Apostles chapter 15), Peter, James, and Paul determined that Gentiles could become Christians without first becoming Jews. Paul on Mars Hill in Athens preached in Greek about an unknown God already worshiped by the Athenians.

No one normative model of worship can be discovered in church history either. In the fourth century, Augustine most often preached on the front steps of his cathedral in Carthage, engaging the best rhetoricians of his age in debate, then invited people to enter the doors of the church for the sacraments. "Opening the doors of the church," a standard phrase to describe the evangelistic task of the church, may, in part, be attributed to Augustine's physically opening the outer doors of his cathedral to the unchurched seekers standing in Carthage's forum. The Western church's lectionary developed in the fourth century as a systematic way to witness to a newly Christianized Roman world. When many Romans became Christian under the Roman emperor Constantine, the lectionary kept alive the whole biblical story. For the untrained masses, the story of Jesus was entirely repeated every year. The great stained-glass windows of the European cathedrals pictured the story of Jesus to people who could not read or understand the Latin texts, while the mystery plays of the late Middle Ages told the gospel story through raucous skits acted by characters outside church walls.

Re-forming liturgy continued. Martin Luther rebelled against seven sacraments and wrote the Deutsche Messe (the service of Holy Communion), composed hymns, and translated the whole of Scripture into German so people could understand the gospel.[9] The 1580 Lutheran Formula of Concord, one of the definitive statements of the Protestant Reformation, declared that "we further believe, teach, and confess that the community of God in every place and at every time has the right, authority, and power to change, to reduce, or to increase ceremonies according to its circumstances."[10] Likewise, the Anglican Articles of Religion, adapted by John Wesley in 1784, declared that "it is a thing plainly repugnant to the Word of God, and Custom of the Primitive Church, to have Publick Prayer in the Church, or to minister the Sacraments in a Tongue not understood by the People."[11] John Wesley, in his own words, "agreed to become more vile" by preaching and celebrating the sacraments outdoors. The Methodists in England built chapels, not churches, for common folks. Charles Wesley wrote hymns that were not acceptable to seventeenth-century Anglicans because he gleaned many tunes from popular culture. General William Booth, a man of the Wesleyan tradition and the founder of the Salvation Army, put bands of musicians on the streets for the poor, declaring, "Why should the Devil have all the good tunes?" The camp meetings on the American frontier created new spaces and traditions uniquely adapted to that newly forming culture. The church universal's own tradition calls congregations to recraft established patterns and establish new styles of worship.

Liturgical balance between text and context, between gospel and setting, is a long-standing Christian theological position and constitutes our history. What, then, are the implications for contemporary worship? Today radically new contexts and changing generations require radically fresh retelling of the gospel. And so it has always been. As Susan White writes, "The great ages of faith and renewal for Christian worship have been those that were most unstable. . . . Renewal happens when people 'break away from the dead hands and dead minds of the past, and are able to see and think creatively.' "[12]

At present, the church at worship must primarily embody Christ by meeting new generations of people in new cultures with the eternally pertinent good news of God's coming in Jesus Christ. Jesus calls his disciples to serve one another as he served them. In too many congregations, worship has become the altar which people must stand back from and revere, rather than an aisle along which people are invited to walk. Serving people and their needs with the gospel and offering them the means of grace through patterns and styles appropriate to their context are most important. Arbitrary determination of one unchanging pattern brings about the loss of communicative skill. The worship of God by a transformed (and transforming) people is the goal we seek.

Primary Questions

The goal of all this theological talk is to provoke questions; they are typically more important than answers. This theological discussion raises several primary questions, and congregations must start by asking the right ones.

The first question must be: Which God do we proclaim? Other ways of asking the question include: What is God's grace? How is this grace expressed? What is it that the church has to present? This question raises the issue of theological integrity and the answer is clear: the church must present God and God's grace as embodied in the ministry and life of Jesus Christ. God's grace is Christ Jesus, this one who comes to all creation in self-giving, one who lives and dies for others. This gospel must be the message.

The next question must be: How shall the church present this eternal message to a particular community in a way that evokes response? Other ways to ask this include: Which particular people need the transforming message? To whom can the church speak the good news? Who will hear what the church presents? Will worship transform lives? What is the most effective worship for a particular congregation? What style of worship effects a new relationship between God in Jesus Christ and God's people in this specific place and time? These questions draw attention to the issue of vitality. The answers will vary radically in every congregation and every community of faith. All these questions presuppose that there is no one right way to worship, but there are effective and ineffective ways to worship; ineffective worship does nothing, while effective worship transmits transforming grace.

Unfortunately, too many worship leaders reviewing their worship ask other questions first. Such wrong questions include: Which style of worship is best? Which pattern of worship is most Christian? What new things should we do or not do in worship? These questions imply that there is one right style of worship, or that God prefers one pattern to another, or that any one act of worship may or may not be necessarily Christian. The fundamental issue—whether a particular presentation of the gospel is relevant to a particular audience—too often goes unaddressed.

Wesleyan liturgical theology fundamentally requires an openness to new patterns of worship. Wesleyan worship evokes transformation—transformation of women, men, children, and youth—by God's grace. The goal of worship is to effect a new relationship between God and each person and the whole community gathered. It is not to be ritually correct or emotionally manipulative. Understanding the gospel and its call to share the Word of God and having clarity about who will be served means that a congregation and its worship leaders must make decisions about patterns and styles of worship. The goal is integrity and vitality joined together in effective worship. Effective styles of worship are found whenever new persons are reached with the saving grace of God. At these moments of human transformation through the grace of Jesus Christ, God is truly glorified.

5 | ENRICHING WORSHIP: FIRST STEPS FIRST

A worship committee gathers in the church library. Around the table sit the pastor, the part-time musician, the volunteer pianist, the altar guild chair, a new young adult member, a long-time member of the choir, and a college student home for the holidays. The formal agenda is to plan worship for Lent and Easter. The unspoken agendas are more critical: worry about declining worship attendance, anxiety about lack of resources, concern about new music and how long the old organ will last, distress about the furniture being moved, hope that new people will be reached, fear of alienating the existing congregation, and impressions that the whole of worship is irrelevant. The conversation quickly shifts away from the Ash Wednesday service. Questions arise: What can we do to excite people? Why can't we sing just the old hymns? Who moved the communion table? Who wants to sing this new music? Why can't we get visitors to come back a second time? Why aren't we trying something radical? By the end of the session, everyone is tense and no progress is made.

Worship leaders and congregations must respond to new generations and new audiences with new expressions of worship. Sensitive and responsive liturgy is our Christian tradition. No one pattern of worship serves every generation. The way a congregation chooses to worship with baby boomers may well serve that generation, but that very worship pattern will need to change again as new generations emerge or new audiences are identified. The old saying is true: whoever marries the ethos of one age will become a widow in the next. What worked with the builder generations is not working with the boomers, nor will worship specifically for boomers serve well the busters and millennials. The gospel demands new cultural sensibilities to engage every new generation.

Resisting worship reform ensures demise. Doing nothing guarantees that any congregation with any one fixed pattern of worship will increasingly serve a smaller and smaller proportion of society. Since the 1950s, while the Methodist Church (and then The United Methodist Church) has used primarily Liturgical services to serve the builder generations, membership has declined in North America from 6 percent of the population to 3 percent of the population. The memberships of all other mainline denominations parallel this precipitous decline. Overall, the percentage of persons attending any worship service on a regular basis has also steadily fallen. Can worship for new generations reverse this decline?

Evangelism, sharing the good news of Jesus Christ, demands that the church offer the gospel through multiple patterns and styles of worship. A passion for sharing the gospel with new people demands new approaches to worship. The mission of the church is not to perpetuate any one style of worship but to convey the transforming grace of Jesus Christ to new generations.

A Strategy for Enriching Worship

Many established congregations are now considering changing, supplementing, and enriching their worship to reach the unchurched/seekers/prechurched or other audiences such as boomers, busters, or millennials. Too many times, unfortunately, leaders and congregations start making changes too quickly. The idea is that if a congregation adds choruses or a drama or any other changes to worship, then some new person will attend worship. Such a goal is almost never achieved. The reason for such a failure is that quick changes, while made with good intentions, have no clarity of direction or purpose; the leaders are uncertain where the worship is going or why. Such a journey of worship reform is like going on a trip without a road map or a clear destination.

There are some first steps that must occur prior to making any decision about which worship pattern is appropriate in any particular congregation. Take the correct first steps first. The following offers one approach to worship reform and renewal: create a worship team, ask questions, name a vision, and define an audience. Worship reform and renewal cannot be rushed or treated lightly, but change can happen if these first steps are initiated.

Form a Worship Team

The creation, leadership, and evaluation of worship must be the work of a worship team: pastors, musicians, and other laity or professionals directly responsible for worship in a local congregation. While a whole congregation must agree and work together when worship is reformed, ultimate responsibility for suggestions, guidance, and enactment rests on a worship team. Without leaders working together, worship will have limited impact. Contemporary worship requires of worship leaders more skills and expertise than ever before. Knowing how to read an official book of worship or hymnal is not enough. No one person has all the skills necessary; lone wolves will not survive. Good worship requires a corporate vision, energy, and mutual support.

Pastors are the first among equals on a worship team. Pastors typically have more training in worship, and typically are administratively responsible for worship as a whole. These ordained leaders must initiate worship evaluation and be central in a worship team. If the pastor is willing to work on worship reform, the process will succeed; if the pastor is unwilling or unable to give key guidance, reform will fail.

The first step that clergy must make is to recruit the best available persons to serve on a worship team. Each person must come with particular skills that will enhance worship: musicians, artists, dramatists, singers, and others who will strengthen worship in particular ways. No one person has all the skills and talents needed to lead effective contemporary worship of any style. Pastors must then train and guide a worship team. The pastor-in-charge has to be wholly committed to leading a team and congregation and exceptionally capable of doing so. All of this is required of pastors, but only with others can they bring about more effective worship.

Musicians are the second most important leaders of worship reform within a worship team. Musicians are critical because music is the key to every pattern of contemporary worship. When the music works, the service works; when the music simply limps along or fails, the worship fails completely. Music serves as the primary evangelistic tool of the church to serve existing persons and to reach new audiences. The music revolution on TV and radio encourages music that is accessible and memorable, and church musicians must seek out such music that is biblical and simple and expresses emotions. While pastors must initiate and support change, often musicians must lead the way.

Adding a qualified and competent musician to a worship team may of necessity cost more money. Musicians increasingly are not volunteers but paid professionals, but money invested in a musician is money well spent. Rarely is one musician able to lead a Liturgical service and a Praise and Worship service and a Seeker service. Increasingly, congregations are hiring multiple musicians to serve multiple worship services. A classically trained organist may be best for hymns, while a young adult self-taught at the keyboard may be best for choruses. Not every musician needs to be paid, but a paid leader will attract competent volunteers to complement the musical program. Congregations committed to finding and paying appropriate musicians will succeed. Those congregations who hope to get by with volunteers only will have limited success. Invest in good musicians and add them to a team.

Pastors and musicians must then include others on a team: choir directors, singers, readers, dramatists, altar guild members, communion stewards, artists, dancers, and others with special gifts. Worship teams are not the place to put people who "represent" one group or another; such representative persons often become proponents of serving only one current segment of an existing congregation. Rather, a team must consist of people who have a significant role to play in active worship leadership. This total team may consist of as few as three people but no more than ten persons.

With the creation of any worship team, the work begins. The task of leading worship should start with team members experiencing more variety in worship. Looking for new experiences of worship should include studying more seriously all the hymnals and books of worship now available. Wonderful resources are already on bookshelves and provide excellent suggestions for reinvigorating, for example, essential liturgies like Holy Communion and Baptism and for exploring anew ancient rites such as services of healing. Start with what is already available on the bookshelf. Most learning, however, will not come from print, video, or denominational resources.

Each member of the team will have specific things he or she each needs to learn. Pastors must primarily learn more about music and trust their musicians. Musicians must primarily expand their experiences beyond denominational hymnals and the classic repertoire of the church. They must create new music, try contemporary Christian choruses, Taize music, and secular music. In this quest, musicians must widen the range of the publishers and distributors they use, and move from organ and piano to new instruments. Other members of a team will also need to stretch their horizons.

But a team must then look further. Team members will all need to experience for themselves alternative forms of worship. They must worship in other congregations, especially growing congregations in their own area or other congregations that worship effectively with a specific group of people. Attendance at church conferences such as those held at Willow Creek, Community of Joy, Crystal Cathedral, and others where leaders in training learn from the skilled practitioners will be invaluable. Learn from worship leaders who have already forged new paths.

A commitment to planning together is another critical quality of any effective worship team. For example, when planning new services, the leader of a team, probably the pastor, must identify every new service for at least the next three months, name its day and date, establish the Scripture text or theme of that service, and write down the focus in a clear, declarative sentence. Focus on what particular concern or need of the congregation will be addressed. Then share these plans with everyone on the planning team. The team together should then select music, choruses, visuals, dramas, and everything else about the service. Share this information with the whole congregation and invite others to participate also. Good planning is essential.

In the midst of this learning and planning, a worship team must eliminate its fear of change and prepare a congregation for change. Change is scary; worship experiences never before tried are frightening. Fear is the initial and greatest hurdle to leap before worship changes. Change is difficult in the best of situations. Abraham and Sarah, who set out for a new land not knowing precisely where that journey would lead, provide role models. Abraham and Sarah knew their guide and followed with faithful trust. Present-day churches must do the same. For example, older congregations must overcome their fear of the young and be willing to invest time, money, and staff to reach new generations. The builder generations must passionately want their children and grandchildren to have faith. The vast majority of older established churches, unfortunately, will be resistant and fearful and thus refuse to attempt this hurdle. But for the few congregations who risk change and overcome their fear, great blessings can follow.

Courage to experiment is another quality necessary for any worship team. A team must be willing to try some new things, play new music, show a video, offer a drama, set aside the robes, unplug the organ, or play a new instrument. God created everything and called it good, thus the church must learn to use all that God has provided. Each team must be enabled to acknowledge and respond to God's gracious presence in worship in creative ways.

Having experimented, every team must anticipate the possibility of failure. Not everything will work. But what is "failure"? Failures follow even efforts to be faithful. Not everyone will like the new music. Most people in existing congregations will prefer the style of worship they already know. Not every piece of equipment will work the way leaders planned. But failure is acceptable. Paul failed with the Athenians, even when he tried to speak in ways culturally relevant. He learned, then moved on to Corinth. Wesley failed in Georgia, and in retreat from his failure learned from the Moravians. The Ladies Bible Class may revolt the first time a congregation sings choruses via an overhead projector in the sanctuary. Occasional failure is inevitable. Learn from the mistakes and try again. Do not fall back to fear.

And finally, a team must constantly evaluate and try again. Learn what went wrong. Then, listen, learn, and listen some more. Listen to God's vision, overcome fear, plan some more, and experiment again. Every experience is a building block for more effective worship.

This first step—creating a team that learns together, plans, experiments, risks failure, evaluates, and experiments again—is fundamental to effective worship that communicates the gospel.

Ask Questions

Having created a worship team committed to working together, before any changes are made the next stage in reforming and renewing worship is to ask the right questions. Prior to making any changes in worship, a worship team, as well as each worship leader and the whole congregation, must ask itself, and have clear answers to, the following questions:

Are we open to God's grace?
Are we willing to share the gospel with other people?
Are we willing to seek out and serve new people beyond those we already serve?
Do we have a passion for the unchurched/seekers/prechurched?
Do we understand that worship is the primary way to reach new people?
Are we willing to listen as new people critique our worship?
Are we willing to try new styles and patterns of worship to reach out?
How much will we risk to reach out to others?
What aspects of our worship are nonnegotiable?

What or who is the final authority as we make our
   decisions?
Are we willing to invest the time, money, and skill needed
   to change?
Will our new worship reflect what we believe?[1]

Each of these questions needs carefully considered
answers; answers that are owned and adopted by all the
worship leaders. Answers to these questions will determine
whether a congregation will offer revitalized worship or
simply continue to worship in ineffective patterns.

As a worship team addresses these questions, it must not
be satisfied with easy questions or answers. One important
question is, Are we willing to invest a congregation's limited resources in starting a new service at worship? Starting
a new service may require hiring an additional musician,
purchasing an electronic keyboard, running the furnace
another day a week, allowing the pastor more time each
week for worship planning (and thus less time for home
visitation), and so on. Too many congregations have too
quickly started a new service, not counting the cost, and
then abandoned the service two months later.

Having answered these questions, worship teams, leaders, and congregations may then decide to change or add to
or simply reaffirm existing patterns of worship.

Create a Vision

The creation of a vision or mission statement is the third
essential ingredient for significant worship renewal. Until a
worship team (and its congregation) can identify its central
vision, there can be no clarity about which direction to go.
If one does not care where one is going, then any road will
take one there. If, however, one does have a direction, then
which roads to follow are clear. The Community of Joy
vision statement defines its entire ministry and especially

its worship: "That all may know Jesus Christ and become responsible members of his church, we share his love with joy inspired by his Holy Spirit." This vision statement clearly identifies that reaching new persons and making them disciples of Jesus through joyful worship is their focus. Every worship team must have a MISSION—*M*emorable, *I*nspirational, *S*criptural, *S*piritual, *I*nvitational, *O*utreaching, and *N*otable—statement.

One critical task of a vision statement is to remind worship teams, leaders, and congregations that worship is a missionary effort. The evangelistic task of offering Christ, spreading scriptural holiness, and reforming the land must shape worship. In the tradition of John Wesley, worship is primarily a means through which human lives are transformed by God's grace. While it is important to honor God through worship directed to God, God is even more honored by transforming human lives through the Word, water, bread and cup, prayer, and fellowship. Congregations must begin by seeing worship as the primary opportunity to feed new persons the transforming gospel. As Bishop D. T. Niles, a Methodist bishop from Sri Lanka, once wrote: "Evangelism . . . is one beggar telling another beggar where to get food."[2]

Name an Audience

The final, and most difficult, of these first steps is naming an audience to serve. In the recent past, "marketing" has become a specific field of knowledge intimately related to service—communicating information about a product to a specific audience in a specific context. While marketing language offends some leaders, churches should well consider treating members and nonmembers as persons with integrity, as the subjects of our love and concern and service, or in marketing language, as our customers.

Most church leaders, unfortunately, still think of their current church people as members of a club who are expected to obey, contribute to an ongoing operation, and be satisfied with whatever ministry is provided. The church becomes an end in itself. Vital Christian congregations in their worship must see each current or potential member as a person with specific spiritual needs to be served. Too many congregations are concerned primarily with the sheep that are already in the sheep pen rather than being passionately interested in the sheep beyond the pen's gates. All baptized Christians must see their ministry as a holistic evangelistic ministry to the world.

Such a marketing perspective does not imply that followers of Jesus must only or always be customers of God's grace. Where people begin their walk with Jesus is not the place either God or the church anticipates that they will end. Not everyone who first heard Jesus followed. Everyone who did follow, however, was taught the path of servanthood. Conversion fundamentally changes people from persons being served into persons who serve others. In Christian language, hearers become servants; in marketing language, customers become suppliers. The goal of all effective worship is to begin meeting people's most basic needs, with the Christian hope that they will become committed followers of the Way and serve others as Christ has served them. But seekers cannot become servants if the church does not first reach out to them.

Every congregation serves a specific audience, either by choice or by default. Despite claims to the contrary, no one congregation or denomination serves everybody. A popular myth—because the gospel is for everyone, every congregation ought to serve everyone—is simply naive. No single congregation reaches equally well the poor and the rich, young and old, persons of all colors, the educated and uneducated, seekers and believers, or persons whose primary language varies. Worship teams and congregations must start evaluating their worship by asking specifically with whom they work and how they hope to lead these people into becoming disciples of Jesus Christ.

There are at least five audiences in any congregation's worship, and worship may either effectively (succeed in changing one's relationship with God) or ineffectively (fail to initiate a change in one's relationship with God) serve all five audiences. The first audience is the current members, those people who attend worship regularly. Effective worship will be designed primarily to be a vehicle to enrich regular members with sanctifying grace, to enable persons to move toward being perfect in love. Ineffective worship will seek primarily to please, or more often not offend, those people who now attend.

The second audience is church officials, those members of the official boards of a church or the informal gatekeepers who control a congregation. Effective worship for these persons will acknowledge and deepen their servant ministry. Ineffective worship will pander to them, so that if a vocal administrative board member objects to a particular aspect of worship, that act of worship disappears.

The third audience is the congregational staff, both volunteers and paid employees. Too often they see themselves as the primary audience. For example, when a musician chooses only hymns that the musician believes to be good music or a pastor refuses to preach on a particular text, each has shifted from serving to being served. Effective worship to staff members enables them to express their faith and serve others at the same time.

The fourth audience is the suppliers, those who reflect denominational interests such as diocesan officials, bishops, supervising pastors, and official agencies of a denomination with their guidance and official documents. These people are not a part of the particular worshiping congregation, but they exercise influence from a distance. When a congregation uses a hymnal's order of worship slavishly, the congregation has served its denomination first and has created ineffective worship.

These last two groups, staff and suppliers, while a vital part of any community, should never be a primary audience of any congregation.

The fifth audience—the most overlooked, yet important, audience for any congregation—is the unchurched/seekers/prechurched in its local community. Every community is filled with persons marginalized from the dominant culture and overlooked by most congregations. As a result these persons are truly strangers to the gospel. While new audiences may be considered geographically, demographically, culturally, or spiritually, generational divisions appear to be the most profound factor when identifying these persons. While many people in a community are indifferent to the church, many others are yet seeking. Most congregations never see their worship through the eyes of these outsiders. Congregations ignore these seekers in their community and thus close their doors to all except their internal, preexisting members, church leaders, staffs, and denominational officials. God is always searching for persons, like a shepherd looking for a lost sheep, a woman looking for a lost coin, or a father looking for his son. A primary audience for any congregation must be these seekers.

Seekers looking for the gospel are all around us. Belmont United Methodist Church in Nashville, Tennessee, is located just down the street from Vanderbilt University. This university attracts many international students, especially from Africa and Asia. Many of these students, knowing absolutely nothing about Christianity, frequently come to Belmont for worship. They want to learn more about North American culture and, secondarily, to explore Christianity. A fascinating task at Belmont has been and continues to be to interpret the gospel to those who know nothing about the Bible, Jesus Christ, or current beliefs and practices of Christians. Where to begin? What to say first? How does its worship reflect its beliefs? How does its worship tell Jesus' story to new people? What is crucial for Belmont and for every congregation to remember is that such seekers are not just from overseas; they are now the majority in every neighborhood.

All five of these groups are legitimate audiences, and all have a right to be served. What each congregation must do, however, is to keep in balance the variety of needs of all these diverse audiences. Congregations, however, that serve only the first four audiences—current members, lay leaders in the congregation, staff, and denominational leaders—fail in their mission and will cease to exist. Every person in these existing groups will move away, join another church, or die. There is no significant future in continuing to serve only present members. Only those congregations that serve the unchurched seekers in a specific community will survive for another generation. Most established congregations have declined because they have become comfortable with their current constituents, a base that is constantly declining. The only viable alternative is for the older generations to care passionately for the younger generations. Grandparents and parents must be as concerned, or even more concerned, about their children's and grandchildren's relationship with God as their own. Older neighbors must care passionately about the spiritual amnesia of their younger neighbors. The rise of distinct new patterns of contemporary worship reflects an intentional effort by some congregations to reach the unchurched of the new generations.

Once a worship team identifies an audience, a team must listen carefully to that audience. The food to satiate their hunger comes in many forms. The assembled worship team must attune their ears, eyes, and hearts to their specific, identified audience and learn what people both desire and need. In every community, there are many different people with many different needs. What people needed last year is different from what is needed now and different from what will be needed next year. Ask what books people read, what television shows they watch, what political forces offend and gratify, what is happening to their families, and so forth. The list of books in the annotated bibliography at the back of this book also provides a number of insights into a number of generational audiences; read and learn from these books. Until a team knows intimately the gospel and the people to be served they cannot design worship.

This requirement to listen is not an appeal to give people only what is easy and satisfying. Listening to what struggles people face and should face, what fears they confront and should confront, and what concerns they deal with daily and should deal with daily provides the context in which the grace of God must be proclaimed. At times grace must answer, and at other times, grace must challenge. But before speaking, listen.

The goal of listening will help clarify where worship will go. The destination may be to encourage individuals and/or strengthen the church universal. The music may be what is found in the official denomination resources and/or in other resources. Music in a congregation may include choruses and/or traditional hymns. Many congregations that had abandoned hymns altogether have now returned to hymns for part of their worship life. Listen carefully before jumping to easy answers.

Congregations must look carefully at their local communities. But be careful. Some persons believe that the only appropriate audience is younger generations, and that only large membership congregations can survive. By paying attention, however, to the main question—How shall we present God's grace in Jesus Christ to a particular community in a way that evokes response?—any congregation in any setting can spread the gospel.

In Charlotte, North Carolina, a large number of younger persons and families have migrated to the university area.

A number of older, more established congregations in the same area essentially welcome the newcomers only if the newcomers convert to the already existing worship patterns. Most of the established congregations have grown only modestly in their worship attendance. At the same time, a number of new congregations are emerging in the same neighborhoods. Created by the Baptists, United Methodists, Presbyterians, and independent congregations, these new congregations recognize and serve a young, educated population, most of whom have had no previous connection with the gospel. Each of these new congregations has created comfortable worship space, adequate parking, programs for children and youth, and, most important, worship that speaks the gospel directly to these seekers and hearers. The worship attendance in these congregations is tremendous. While the patterns and styles vary, all of the new congregations share the gospel well.

But not all congregations need to be like these urban congregations. Several years ago, Linville United Methodist Church was dying. In the shadow of Grandfather Mountain in North Carolina, the congregation lost membership every year. Almost every member of the church was over sixty years old. Yet the church dreamed of attracting new, younger members. They renovated a classroom into a nursery, staffed it every week, and waited for the children and their parents to come. None did. The difficulty was that there were almost no young couples with children in the community. Rather, the community was increasingly populated by retired older adults who lived in the mountains only during the summer. In a bold move, the congregation determined that they would serve this growing, older population. They dismantled the nursery and created a lending library of large-print books. Each entryway became handicap accessible. Worship reflected a style with which this population was comfortable, such as singing hymns primarily in the southern gospel tradition. And people came, and the church grew and still thrives. When any congregation opens its eyes to its community, recognizes unmet needs, and shares the gospel in new ways, God will bless the work.

Contemporary culture is, if anything, rushed. Too many people like to make quick decisions and take fast action. In worship, quick decisions and fast action almost always fail. Take some time. Establish a worship team. Ask questions. Name a vision. Select a target audience and listen to that audience. Take these steps slowly and deliberately. Then, when the journey toward worship reform and renewal has begun, it is time to begin talking about specific changes in worship.

6 FOUR CORNERSTONES

n any given community, the majority of established congregations have settled on a low plateau or are in decline. Their worship is created mostly by one or two individuals, who know all the answers, who lack any clear vision, and who cannot identify any particular audience to serve. The congregations have not just plateaued or begun to decline in terms of numbers of people who attend worship; they are failing to share the gospel with new people and to form fully committed disciples of Jesus Christ.

The primary challenge to the majority of established congregations is simple: How can they share the gospel with new generations to form followers of Jesus Christ? In many established congregations, worship, primarily Liturgical, appears remote and hostile to outsiders. Much of the evidence available indicates that new generations are rejecting many aspects of the worship found in established congregations. How can established congregations worship to reach new generations with gospel integrity and faithfulness to human needs?

Taking the first steps first—creating a worship team, asking the right questions, naming a vision, and identifying an audience—is not by itself enough. The first steps are not the only steps that must be taken on the road to effective worship. Liturgical congregations can now seriously strengthen their current worship practices and patterns in three ways. The first way to reform and strengthen worship is by emphasizing the foundational elements of worship. Congregational worship can become significantly more faithful to both the gospel and new generations when worship takes seriously the Word of God, the sacraments, prayer, and fellowship. An emphasis on these four cornerstones of worship is the focus of this chapter. The following chapter will discuss two additional ways to strengthen worship: by creating a new service of worship that intentionally seeks to attract new people and by blending together elements from Liturgical, Praise and Worship, and Seeker services. The goal of these suggestions, however, is not just change for the sake of change. Change in and of itself is neither good nor bad. The goal of all three patterns of worship is renewal: revitalizing congregational worship for the sake of the gospel.

The Cornerstones

The first way to reform worship is to reemphasize the foundations of worship: the Word of God, the sacraments, prayer, and fellowship. The style, language, instruments, media, music, vestments, setting, and every other aspect of worship may change, but four essential elements of worship must never be neglected: the Word of God read aloud, proclaimed, and heard; the sacraments of Baptism and Holy Communion rightly taught and practiced; prayer offered and affirmed; and fellowship in the community by word and sign. Based on patterns of worship from the earliest church, these four components have been emphasized in every revival of the church from Augustine's outreach in Carthage to the Reformation in Europe to the Wesleyan revival in England (these four cornerstones are John Wesley's instituted means of grace) to the camp meetings on the American frontier to all the effective congregations thriving in North American culture today.

What is surprising to both newly emerging and established congregations is that these cornerstones for revitalized worship are found in and stand at the heart of Liturgical worship. These elements are not alien to established congregations; the resources first needed for effective contemporary worship are already available. What inhibits effective contemporary worship in many established congregations is simply a lack of a regular and consistent emphasis on all four of these essential elements.

These cornerstones of worship are clearly expressed in the current hymnals and books of worship of the established denominations (Episcopal, Lutheran, Presbyterian, United Church of Christ, and United Methodist, among others). All of these hymnals and books of worship are serious and thoughtful attempts to express the Christian faith in ways faithful both to the present day and to the traditions of the church universal. While some of these resources are more successful than others in speaking to contemporary culture, they all are rich depositories that have not yet been fully mined. In the movement toward contemporary worship, unfortunately, there is a tendency to discard these hymnals and books of worship and, even worse, their essential elements.

Worship teams and leaders looking for valid forms of contemporary worship must not forget the resources that have sustained the church for centuries; being contemporary does not mean simply throwing away past treasures. In the midst of the massive change now sweeping through worship forms, it is too easy to overlook these foundation stones of worship. To do this, however, not only rejects a rich liturgical heritage, but also submits the church to the tyranny of personal and transient fads. The first way to revitalize worship to reach seekers and strengthen believers is by emphasizing these four foundation stones.

The Word of God

The Word of God read, proclaimed, and heard must be the touchstone of every service of Christian worship: Liturgical, Praise and Worship, and Seeker. Every worship service centers on the Word of God, and so the Word of God should remain central.

A strength of many Praise and Worship and Seeker services is that they begin with an acknowledgment of real-life situations and a focus on contemporary issues facing individuals and the community. The issues range from divorce to how to pray to managing money to how to share the Christian faith with children. If services start with human life, however, leaders must remember that it is the Word of God alone that provides the answers. Ultimately, pop psychology and current fads are not salvific. Karl Barth, a Swiss theologian, advised that preachers should keep the Bible in one hand and the newspaper is the other. Barth's advice remains sound.

How can the Word become more visible in contemporary worship? The Bible itself must be visible, seen, and used in Christian worship, not as an icon or idol, but as the source of the revelation of God's Word for all people. Flashing biblical passages on a screen is not an adequate alternative to holding a Bible in one's hand and reading the Word of God aloud. When the Word is visible only for a moment and then gone, the Bible's momentary presence encourages people to see the Word as simply a visual prop. Using the Book itself encourages the people to read the Book.

The richness and fullness of the Bible must be opened to the people. Do not throw out the lectionary (especially the *Revised Common Lectionary*) too quickly. Too many Praise and Worship and Seeker services use only a small fraction of the Scriptures, predominantly the Gospels and Epistles. The danger is that contemporary preachers will create their own small sacred text from within the Bible, an idiosyncratic canon within the canon of the Old and New Testaments. These pastors forget and thus enable their congregations to forget the height, depth, and breadth of the Scriptures.

The value of the lectionary is its holistic nature. As a congregation follows the Christian year from Advent to Pentecost, it hears the whole of Jesus' story: anticipation of the Messiah, his birth, manifestation, baptism, transfiguration, passion, death, resurrection, and ascension and the coming of the Holy Spirit upon the community of faith. As the lectionary continues, the whole of Scripture from throughout the Old and New Testaments engages believers, new hearers, and seekers, and urges those who hear it to form themselves in the image of Christ.

The lectionary itself took definitive form in the fourth century precisely to form new hearers in the newly Christianized Roman world. Following the advent of the emperor Constantine in the early fourth century, Christianity became increasingly dominant in the Roman world. The pagan people of the Empire began adopting this newly respectable religion, often without learning enough about it. What these new Christians lacked was understanding of and information about their new faith; they were just like seekers today. As the church attempted to teach these new Christians the story of Christ and its meaning for their lives, the church developed the lectionary as the primary means of teaching the whole of the faith. The lectionary told about the mighty acts of God over the course of one year, and then repeated the same basic story year after year until the gospel story become a part of everyone's story.

Today, because many believers and especially seekers are unaware of the riches of Scripture, the lectionary may well prove to be one of the most important traditions for the church to continue. It is remarkable how often the lectionary's chosen text of the day will deal with contemporary issues otherwise not considered. While leaders may not wish to use all three lessons and the psalm from the lectionary each week, using one lectionary text a week as the basis of worship maintains a strong biblical foundation. For example, during the two Christ-centered cycles—Advent/Christmas/Epiphany and Lent/Easter/Pentecost—all three lessons and the psalm revolve around the Gospel reading. On these Christ-centered Sundays, start with the Gospel lesson. During Ordinary Times, the Season after the Epiphany and the Season after Pentecost that stand between the two christological cycles, the lessons operate on three semicontinuous tracks and do not have any one central theme or thrust. On these ordinary Sundays, choose any one of the three lessons and start there.[1]

Simply reading scripture, however, is not by itself sufficient for faithful worship. Preaching the Word links the Scriptures with human life. Worship is incomplete without a sermon, however it is delivered, outlined, or related to the music and drama of the day. While a drama or a video clip may complement the Word proclaimed, avoid using drama or video as a substitute for a sermon. Narrative, expository, and didactic preaching/teaching especially, all typical in Praise and Worship and Seeker services, are faithful to scripture texts and engage contemporary audiences. Good preaching always has demanded and still demands personal devotion, serious study, adequate preparation, and close attention to a particular community of faith.

Reading and preaching the Word, however, are still not enough. The Word of God calls forth a response from those who hear. At the end of every service, every individual in the congregation must be able to answer the question "So what?" What difference did the sermon make to each individual? Effective contemporary worship insists that reading and preaching the Word must relate to the listeners. The best of contemporary worship includes time, space, and opportunities for persons to respond following the preaching. For example, after a narrative about Jesus' healing ministry, an effective service should offer an opportunity for a congregation to pray for one another with the laying on of hands and anointing with oil.

Invitations to respond to the Word—a logical, sequential ending to a sermon or a time of teaching—serve as catalysts of a response. They should be personal, specific, clear, and unambiguous. Altar calls, silent prayer, vocal responses, invitations to church membership or to recommitment, prayers of confession, testimonies, hymns, offerings, and a multitude of other responses enable individuals and congregations to answer the call of God. Resist the temptation to let preaching or teaching be presentation alone; instead, encourage hearers to respond to the winsome grace of God.

When believers, new hearers, and seekers hear the Word read and proclaimed, and then are enabled to respond, persons grow as disciples of Christ. The Word of God must be the first foundation stone of effective contemporary worship.

The Sacraments

Baptism and the Lord's Supper are together the second foundation stone of worship. Baptism calls persons into Christian discipleship; the Lord's Supper offers food for the spiritual journey. Some contemporary worship either ignores or minimizes these essential rites of grace by reducing the texts, neglecting the actions, and belittling their significance. Praise and Worship and Seeker services in particular ignore the sacraments. These signal acts of divine intervention must be celebrated in a way that makes them powerful moments in contemporary worship. Through their actions, even more so than their words, these sacraments declare the essential message of salvation. Emphasizing them highlights the heart of the gospel.

Baptism provides individuals and congregations the opportunity to stand against the forces of evil in contemporary culture, publicly profess Jesus Christ as Savior, and commit themselves to Christian service. In the Wesleyan tradition, Baptism washes away original sin, initiates a new covenant with God, admits persons into the church, and makes us children of God and heirs of God's kingdom.[2] The best of contemporary worship emphasizes this turning from evil toward Christ with services filled with water, singing, and testimonies. There is no more powerful visual and aural rite than the washing of a new believer with water, laying on of hands, and praying for the work of the Holy Spirit. Contemporary worship itself stands as a testimony that in each new generation Christians are made, not born. Baptism is the certain sign of one's incorporation into the body of Christ.

The actions of baptism are wonderful means of communicating the gospel story in contemporary services. First, the candidates (or their parents/sponsors in the case of children or others unable to answer for themselves) publicly witness to their faith. This witness may be made through responding to formal questions—"Do you believe in Jesus Christ?"—and/or by offering a personal witness. The congregation then joins the candidate in declaring the apostolic faith, perhaps by reciting or reading the Apostles' Creed, an ancient text declaring the essential beliefs of water-born Christians. The blessing of water reminds people of God's saving acts through water. The prayer of Thanksgiving Over the Water may be read from a book, but this prayer is more effective when pastors learn its trinitarian structure and then pray from the heart. There is no need for either the worship leaders or the congregation to read from a book. Let the prayer be passionate and particular to the person being baptized. Moving away from reading formal liturgies and emphasizing the relational and expressive quality of the rite restores the power of baptism for contemporary people. Finally, during the baptism itself, let the water itself be seen and heard. Thoroughly wash the candidates; get the newly baptized wet!

Several smaller actions help reemphasize baptism in a contemporary service. Baptize particularly on special holy days, such as the Baptism of the Lord, Easter, Pentecost, and All Saints Day to link an individual's baptism with the larger story of God's activity in history. Build baptismal pools and fonts large enough to be seen; install a fountain in the pools to enable people to hear running water. Keep the baptismal pool or font continually in view of every member of a congregation as a constant reminder of the sacrament. Encourage parents of children or sponsors of adult converts to personally introduce the candidates to the congregation. Finally, clothe baptismal candidates with new clothes or light a baptismal or Christ candle to reinforce the new presence of God in the life of the baptized. However, while these secondary signs can become positive witnesses to the new life in Christ, leaders must be cautious that they do not eclipse the primary action of washing with water.

The rediscovered rituals of baptismal reaffirmation can well become powerful evangelistic events in the life of any contemporary congregation. In such services, used when no persons are to be baptized, confirmed, or received into the church, the whole congregation renounces Satan, accepts anew Jesus Christ as Savior, and affirms the faith. Then with liturgical acts other than baptism—lifting water for all to see, sprinkling water toward the people, or, best of all, inviting persons to touch the water or to touch the water to their heads or hearts—people reaffirm their baptismal relationship to God. Singing choruses during a reaffirmation increases its impact. Baptismal reaffirmation thus involves sound, sight, and touch in a service that engages both the heart and mind.

The Eucharist (or Holy Communion, Lord's Supper, Divine Liturgy, Mass, Holy Meal, or Jesus' Dinner Party) is the primary response by the community to the Word of God read and proclaimed; and so it should remain in any pattern of contemporary worship. The meal is a memorial of Christ's actions, a means of conveying God's grace to all, a sacrifice of Christ and those who believe, and a stimulus to future hope. The Lord's Supper is clearly an invitation to seekers to be in community with our Savior and other believers. In the eating of the bread and drinking from the cup, the people of God truly are in the living presence of Jesus Christ. Because the Holy Meal involves action, fellowship, and food, it clearly fits into contemporary patterns of worship and can be celebrated even more frequently. Increasingly, congregations celebrate the Eucharist weekly, and leaders are still learning from congregations that celebrate the Holy Feast with fervor.

Focusing on the ritual actions of taking, blessing, breaking, and giving the bread and of sharing the cup is the single best way to reemphasize the Holy Meal in a contemporary fashion. Take a whole loaf of bread and large chalice prepared by members of a congregation. Lift the bread and cup toward heaven and offer an extemporaneous yet structured Prayer of Great Thanksgiving to God the Father, the Son, and the Holy Spirit. The variety of Prayers of Great Thanksgiving in all the major prayerbooks offer wonderful examples of how the Prayer may be offered in a structured pattern yet be particular to specific occasions. Contemporary worship leaders must learn the trinitarian model and then speak from the heart; there is no necessity at all for any leader or any member of a congregation to read from a book. Visibly and boldly tear the bread apart. Assign laity to serve the bread and cup. During the giving, sing contemporary choruses. The actions of taking, blessing, breaking, and giving can together declare the essential message of the faith without a single word being spoken.

Smaller actions can dramatically improve how a congregation shares the Holy Meal. Emphasize holy days—First Sunday of Advent, Christmas Eve and Day, the Day of Epiphany, the First Sunday in Lent, Holy Thursday, the Day of Easter, Day of Pentecost, and All Saints' Day as occasions for celebration, linking a congregation's actions with the historic church. Celebrating Holy Communion during weddings and healing services is particularly effective as a contemporary witness of faith. In addition, vary the worship settings; move the Holy Feast to the outdoors, a fellowship hall, or a lakeside; set the table so that everyone may see the bread and cup and all the ritual actions clearly.

Strong contemporary worship emphasizes and celebrates Baptism and Holy Communion to introduce modern believers and seekers to the essential message of the gospel. Through their liturgical actions, the sacraments communicate the heart of the salvation story.

Prayer

Prayer is the third primary means through which all worshipers communicate with God and is another foundation stone of all patterns of worship. Formal (previously prepared as a literary creation) and free (extemporaneous) prayer are both appropriate in any contemporary community gathered to honor God. The historic prayers of the church as well as those composed by the sensitive souls of our time are important means through which any congregation speaks and listens to God. Prayers may be spoken or silent and led by laity or clergy. The prayers may be printed in a bulletin, projected on a screen, or prayed extemporaneously by leader or people. The historic church's corporate prayers prevent the people at worship from falling into self-created ruts or narcissistic pleas for self and family alone, especially when extempore prayer becomes boring and repetitious. Provide variety in substance and style.

Prayer in the congregation should be specific. Generally, long, nonspecific intercessions from the front of a congregation by one individual are unengaging. Rather, worship leaders should solicit specific prayer concerns or encourage worshipers to speak aloud their own concerns, hopes, and dreams. Bidding prayers, when a prayer leader names a particular subject such as prayers for healing and then leaves time for silent prayer, both encourages prayer and teaches seekers, hearers, and believers how to pray.

Other styles of corporate prayer also strengthen the contemporary church. Prayer services are a vital form of corporate worship, taken from the historic church, with great possibilities for the contemporary church. The Services of Daily Praise and Prayer in the *United Methodist Book of Worship* and those found in the Presbyterian *Book of Common Worship* are particularly applicable to worship led by laypersons in homes or settings other than a sanctuary. The psalms, the prayers of the Bible, are wonderful models of corporate prayer. These heartfelt conversations with God often address contemporary needs. Let the saints of the church teach your congregation how to pray. Strongly emphasized in all contemporary services, the priesthood of all believers—the concept that everyone is a priest for others as well as oneself—becomes most visible when congregations create a vital prayer life.

Fellowship

Both believers and seekers grow in grace and faith when they gather with one another to worship. While Seeker services and some Praise and Worship services tend toward presentation, with an emphasis on the congregation as audience, worship should exhibit a congregation's love and deepen their relationships with one another through active participation. Although congregations need to focus on primary audiences, worship most pleases God when it is open to and receives the gifts of people of all ages, conditions, races, and backgrounds. Active participation to develop Christian community is a primary goal of any service of worship.

An important opportunity in contemporary worship is to develop community by using the varied gifts of the community. Worship must not be pastor/leader-centered and -created but God-centered and people-led. At best, worship leaders are prompters of congregational worship, not centers of attention. The talents of artists, dancers, musicians, and dramatists in each community strengthen any service. Fill the sanctuary with the best paraments available. Encourage visual artists to fill the worship space with signs that enhance the message of the day. Dancers should embody the word. Musicians can create music to move the soul. Authors and actors can relate the message in contemporary ways. Every congregation includes many of these artists, but often their gifts are not enlisted to share the gospel. Use the people God has placed in each congregation to speak to the people God has gathered together.

Inclusive language for persons and an expansive language for God are absolutely critical in building community. While many contemporary congregations appear to emphasize the role of men and the masculine qualities of God, contemporary worship at its best celebrates both women and men and recognizes that God cannot be confined to Father, Son, Master, and Lord imagery. Effective worship must make visible the whole people of God, of whatever sex, age, color, abilities, or experiences. God must be named as Father and Mother, caring and strong, majestic and weeping, shepherd and sovereign, and the hundreds of other ways God is named and described in Scripture.

Finally, and most important, music is the single most effective way to bind a community together in fellowship. From plain chant in the cathedrals of Europe to congregational song in brush arbors in the American wilderness to the singing of choruses in large auditoriums, music unites God and persons. Through song, congregations share their faith and experience community with one another and God. Research and encourage music that reflects the spe-

cific musical tastes of a particular congregation. Discover
the vast array of new music being released every week. But,
at the same time, resist the temptation to perform only contemporary music or choruses. Also use the vast range of
music and hymnody from throughout the ages. Do not
assume too quickly that any one audience cares about only
one style of music.

The single best way to build fellowship is to increase the
quantity and quality of music in any service of worship. At
least 40 percent, maybe as much as 60 percent, of an effective service will consist of the best quality music that a congregation can offer. The primary gift of Praise and Worship
is that it balances the sung and spoken word. Planners of
Liturgical services must remember that any act of worship
from an opening Greeting to a closing Benediction may be
sung by a choir or congregation, while a congregation using
Seeker services must work harder at engaging a whole
community through music.

While there is the temptation to discard much of historic
worship, these four cornerstones of worship are essential to
any contemporary service. In the rush toward creative,
experimental, and culturally relevant worship, worship
leaders must be careful not to cast off the past completely.
Do not throw out the baby with the bathwater! Experiment.
Break new ground. Try new patterns of worship. But as a
congregation reforms its worship, do not forget the four
classic foundation stones of worship. Ministry through the
Word, the sacraments, prayer, and fellowship enables God
to call people to discipleship and enables the community
gathered to respond to that call. By emphasizing these four
liturgical contributions of the saints who have sustained the
church for two millennia, the body of Christ will continue
to proclaim God's good news in a new age.

7 NEW SERVICES AND BLENDED WORSHIP

A worship committee gathers again to evaluate its congregation's worship. The members of the committee work well together, know which questions to ask, have a clear vision statement, and have begun focusing on a primary audience. They have also begun to emphasize the Word of God, the sacraments, prayer, and fellowship. Their one Sunday service, a Liturgical service, has become more effective. But still, new generations stay away, hearers pass through but do not remain, and believers appear frustrated. Are there any other approaches to take? What else can a worship team do?

Two additional approaches are also legitimate responses by a worship committee: starting a new service of worship and blending elements from different worship patterns in one service of worship. Starting a new worship service opens up the potential to lead worship in significantly new ways with new groups of people. Other congregations, for a variety of good reasons, decide not to start a new service but transform an existing service by adding some new elements from other styles of worship. Both approaches are appropriate to reach new generations and form new disciples.

Start a New Worship Service

The single most effective way for established congregations to reach new audiences and especially the newer generations is to begin a distinctly different second or third worship service. Starting a new worship service—a Praise and Worship service on Sunday morning or a Seeker service on Saturday night or any other kind of service at any other time—is the best way for a Liturgical congregation to reach out to new communities.

Starting a new service will serve significantly more people than simply reforming or adding new elements to an already established Sunday service. The reasons for a new service's effectiveness are numerous: the new service brings in people who are unable or unwilling to worship at the traditional time, doubles capacity for parking and seating, increases income (through offerings) without increasing expenses significantly (except for music), answers unmet spiritual needs, and offers the possibility for a fundamentally different style of worship without changing an existing worship service. The easiest way to increase average worship attendance and to initiate immediate worship reform and renewal is to start a new service.

The goal is for a congregation to offer some alternative worship options each week. The most successful model is the use of two or three distinct patterns of worship at two or three different times each week. The objective may be to reach seekers with a Seeker service, minister to young believers through a Praise and Worship service, and then care for long-established believers with a Liturgical service.

Begin a new service as if starting a new church. Start with a dream. Does the worship team have a clear vision of what they wish to accomplish? If a team cares about where it is going, then it must have a road map and a destination in mind.

The road will likely be hard. Often beginning a new service makes a current congregation and its leaders feel uncomfortable because it challenges the status quo, brings in new people, and places new demands on the church leaders. New services cost more money, especially for music, and worship leaders have to reorganize their work and schedules dramatically. Fundamentally, leaders and congregations should not attempt to implement a new service without a strong passion and commitment to reaching new people, employing all the gifts available to them, and responding to all the problems these new people will bring.

With a vision in hand, a team must engage in serious long-range planning. Teams that rush into starting a new service while skipping the planning process consistently fail. First and foremost the team must identify who will be responsible for the new service. Do these leaders have the ability, interest, and time to devote to this task? One word of caution: as a team plans, do not start worshiping too soon. It may take six months to a year from the first vision to the first new service.[1]

Next ask, Who will be targeted? Research the community and name a primary audience. What are their needs? Which members of this target audience will help plan and plant this new service? Because of their sheer numbers and their alienation from the gospel, two groups should be especially targeted: unchurched baby busters who have moved to a local community within the past several years and members of the millennial generation.

Identify what pattern of worship will be offered. Once an audience is defined, design worship to share the gospel with that particular audience. Unless the established service is dangerously overcrowded, the style of the new service should be dramatically different from the first. Why? The effort to start a second service is to reach different people, not more of the same kind of folk already being served by the established service. For example, if the established service reaching the builder generation is Liturgical, the new service for boomers might be Praise and Worship. If the first is formal, the new service might be informal. If the first service uses classical hymns and an organ, the second service should consider using choruses and a keyboard. If the first includes clergy in albs, the second service might feature clergy in clothing similar to that of the anticipated congregation.

Determine what day and time of the week to offer this new service. An increasing number of congregations offer their new services on Sunday morning at 11:00, understanding this hour to be the prime time when seekers and the unchurched may look for a congregation. Such a decision means that the established service itself will need a new time, such as earlier on Sunday morning. The way to defend this sort of radical move is to remind the established congregation that the nature of the church is to reach out to new persons rather than to serve the current members. Other communities find that Friday evenings (especially in strong Jewish communities), Saturday evening (in heavily Roman Catholic areas with a tradition of Saturday evening Mass), Sunday afternoons (in college towns), or Sunday evenings (in the Protestant South) work well. Early Sunday mornings are rarely attractive to seekers or younger adults, who are often still in bed; it is rare for an early Sunday service to successfully reach the unchurched.

Another model for a new service is that of a congregation offering two services at the same time but in different spaces. For example, churches like Trinity Methodist Church in Singapore and First Disciples of Christ Church in Lubbock, Texas, offer at 11:00 on Sunday mornings both a Liturgical service in a sanctuary and a Praise and Worship service in a fellowship hall. The two groups of people meet before and after worship in a courtyard or commons area.

One model that should not be followed is that of offering a new service as an occasional substitute to an established service. Some congregations have tried an alternative service, for example, on the first Sunday of the month or on the four fifth Sundays each year. The difficulty is that such occasional new services irritate some church members who still appreciate the established service and frustrate those who want a new service every week. Either start a new service full-time or do not offer it at all.

What about the music in a new service? Praise and Worship and Seeker services, and to a lesser extent Liturgical services, depend more on the musician/worship leader than on the preacher/teacher. New services are primarily defined by their music rather than their pattern of worship or the preaching. Too few musicians, however, have the ability and desire to play, accompany, or direct radically different styles of music. It is unfair and unrealistic to expect one musician to lead multiple styles of worship well. Typically, starting a new service demands hiring or recruiting a new musician specifically for the style of worship chosen. A Praise and Worship musician must know keyboards, drums, computers, and other instruments that will accompany singing, while Seeker service musicians must be able to assemble a band to play for worship. Additionally, new services often require the purchase of new equipment and the use of new technology. Do not start a new service of any style without exceptional musical support.

A new service is also the ideal time for Liturgical congregations to introduce other gifts during worship. Drama skits or video clips may enliven the sharing of the Word. The visuals should be bright and dramatic. The more different the style of worship, the greater the possibility of reaching whole new groups of people. Key to these new gifts, again, is planning. When designing a specific worship service, think at least three months ahead. Choose a scripture passage or theme. Then invite other members of the worship planning team to suggest songs, dances, banners, videos, dramas, skits, or anything else that comes to mind. Enrich the new service by offering elements that appeal to all of the senses.

When the new service begins, commit to a complete and polished worship experience. The very first service is the most important; remember the old adage that you have only one chance to make a first impression. Are all the musicians in place? Do they know the worship pattern? Does the sermon or presentation address a real topic of concern? Is the hospitality gracious? Are complete plans in hand for the next three months? Will multiple worship gifts be offered? Although leaders or a congregation may think of a new service as an "experiment," approach the service as if forming a new community that will continue. Too many congregations indicate that a new service will be "tried" for several weeks and then be evaluated. The problem is that nobody wants to be a part of an experiment. Start with a commitment to worship every week at the same time and place for a given period of time (thirteen weeks or six months or one year). As part of this planning, ensure that the first service will have a critical mass of the target audience at the first service. Members of the established congregation who are similar to the audience sought must commit to support this service throughout its initial introduction.

When a congregation commits to a new service, it must also understand that when a new service is successful new people will place more demands upon the congregation. The nursery will need to be open longer. The Sunday school classes and other small groups will need to expand. The wear and tear on the building will increase. Pastoral demands will increase. Finally, if the service reaches persons who are wholly new to the Christian faith, congregations should be prepared to offer classes on basic Christian beliefs, how to pray, or other topics of primary interest to new followers. New services often create an intense demand for serious spiritual formation in numerous small groups. Plan for the growth pains that success will create.

Finally, be prepared for opposition. An existing worshiping community is rarely happy when a new service of worship begins. Opposition to starting a new service includes arguments that a second service will divide the congregation or create separate congregations within one facility or attract the kinds of people with whom the existing congregation is not comfortable or put too much stress on the facilities. Years after starting a successful new service, most congregations will still regularly hear regrets from longtime members. The truth is that growth does result in creating new communities, new demands, power sharing, and more difficulties. The thing that keeps a congregation together, however many worship services are offered, is the vision and mission of the worship team and congregation. When the vision and mission are to offer Christ to more persons, new services are not divisive but fulfilling.

Blend Worship Patterns

The final way to strengthen worship is to change an existing service into a Blended service. For many established congregations who can only envision one service of worship, Blended worship that combines elements of several patterns is the best solution to serve old and new generations. While all congregations at worship tend toward one or another of the three styles—Liturgical, Praise and Worship, and Seeker—this option weaves these patterns together into one weekly worship service.

The emphasis on blending two or more styles comes from a desire to offer one worship service that serves believers, new hearers, and seekers equally well. These Blended services may combine a Liturgical pattern, contemporary praise choruses, a drama, and print out the creed for the day.[2] Another Blended pattern is a Praise and Worship service that uses several hymns or a more frequent celebration of Holy Communion.[3] Another Blended pattern is a Seeker service that more directly addresses theological issues through exegetical teachings, as in a service that explains a serious theological topic such as substitutionary atonement. The difficulty, however, with all Blended services is that the attempt to serve multiple audiences and agendas often ends up pleasing no one. Blended services are at best an intermediate step to multiple services of worship.

Some persons argue that Blended worship results in "dumbing down" worship. Although blending may seem to be appealing to the lowest set of needs such as singing simple choruses or avoiding reading every lectionary text, the intent is that each service of worship should offer the clearest, highest quality, and most effective encounter with God a congregation can provide to a diverse audience. "Highest quality" and "most effective" does not mean more complicated or arcane rubrics or slavish adherence to any particular pattern of worship. The goal is for worship leaders to clearly understand the gospel they share and the people they address, and seek to bring the two together with every resource available.

As plans develop for a Blended service, always remember that the liturgy must be both relevant and welcoming. Every worship service must be relevant to a particular community, directly addressing concerns of seekers, new hearers, and believers in the gathered community. As worship leaders plan a service, they should always ask, Does this action or word present the gospel? and Who needs this act of worship? In addition, every service must be more welcoming to outsiders. A welcoming Liturgical service, for example, would be easy to follow, being clearly presented through verbal and nonverbal guidance and in a printed worship bulletin that has been designed with visitors in mind.

Remember that no single change or gimmick will lead to success. History is full of the failures of quick fixes. For example, split chancels did not necessarily lead to sacramental vitality, and a changed order of worship did not necessarily lead to worship renewal; likewise, choruses do not necessarily lead to vital singing. Any change must be made in the context of the message to be presented and the audience to whom it is addressed. By concentrating on the gospel and the audience, the forms of worship that are needed for specific groups of people will become much clearer.

Blend Praise and Worship and Seeker Services with a Liturgical Service

While every congregation's worship has a unique style, many possible changes exist that are appropriate for blending specifically Liturgical worship in established congregations with some of the best gifts and insights of Seeker and Praise and Worship services. Some of these suggestions are relatively easy to implement, while others are much more difficult.

Before worship begins:

Establish a theme/topic/text of the day. Focus on one scriptural text or theme. If starting with a scripture, name the central focus of the text in one declarative sentence. If starting with a life situation, name the problem concretely and specifically. Fuzzy topics lead to scattered services. Every part of the service must reinforce this central focus.

Ask the question, So what? What will the primary audience or a particular group of people in a congregation gain from this worship experience? State the primary goal of the day in one declarative sentence, whether it be recommitment, healing, confidence, stronger families, or any other idea.

Simplify the order of worship. Cut, cut, cut everything that does not reinforce the central focus of the day. For example, the Gathering and Sending Forth need not take more than five or ten minutes at the most; a Proclamation followed by an equally strong Response should be the center of a service of the Word, while a Proclamation followed by a powerful Communion with Thanksgiving is the center of a service of Word and Table. Why must a congregation sing the Gloria Patri or use any other part of worship every week? At least one-fourth of all acts of worship can be cut out of the typical Liturgical service without any loss, and in fact, omitting them can significantly strengthen the service.

Improve off-street parking, nursery, restrooms, and directional signs. In a recent survey, these four items ranked above music and preaching for people looking for a new church home. People must be able to park easily, locate the nursery, drop by the restroom, and find the sanctuary before worship begins. Tour the facilities as if you were a first-time visitor to see where problems might lie. An inviting exterior environment creates an inviting worship experience.

Use greeters. Set a goal of having every visitor greeted by at least three people, including the pastor, before worship begins. Encourage gregarious folks to greet people in the parking lot, at every door, and throughout the sanctuary. The pastor should greet visitors in the pews before the service begins.

Use name tags (possibly just first names) for everyone, beginning with current members. Name tags enable everyone to easily see and use people's names. Do not single out, embarrass, or pressure visitors by making them alone wear name tags or raise their hands or stand to introduce themselves. A gracious alternative is for members to stand and then greet those visitors sitting near them.

Eliminate worship bulletins. Bulletins are excellent for announcements about the congregation's life and upcoming events but terrible for establishing eye contact during worship. Revert to hymn boards or purchase overhead/slide/video-data projectors. If a congregation insists on a worship bulletin, make the bulletin easy on the eye and understandable to first-time visitors. Provide the page number of every item of worship including the scripture of the day, the Lord's Prayer, a doxology, and every other act of worship. When using multiple hymnals, indicate which book will be used. List the names of worship leaders, along with other information useful to seekers such as the phone number of the church and which ages of children are welcome in the nursery.

Improve the sound system. Everybody should be able to hear every word of the service clearly. Use an audiotape player to record the service from the back pew as a way of testing the sound system and answer the question, Can everyone hear clearly? If the sound quality is poor, call in a sound expert. New sound systems, as opposed to older systems that simply amplify sound, surround a congregation with softer yet clearer sounds that create an intimate environment.

Improve the lighting. Can everyone see every face and action brightly? Test the lighting by videotaping the service from the back pew. Watch especially for shadows on the faces of worship leaders behind the pulpit, in the choir, and at the font and table. Ask: Can everyone see everything brightly? If not, call an electrician.

Visualize the whole service through the eyes of the congregation. Can everyone in every pew see every aspect of worship and know what is happening? Can they see the baptism of a child or the bread on the table? Videotape a service from a back corner, then watch the videotape with the sound turned off. How effective was the visual impact of the service? Were the banners, vestments, paraments, and all actions distinct and complementary?

Practice reading the Bible before the service begins. Encourage everyone, through the reading, to visualize and understand the text of the day. Readers should take a course in narrative reading. Use a real Bible and give the page number of the passage in the pew Bible. Introduce the passage and its context before the reading. Identify by personal name any character or place that the text refers to with impersonal pronouns.

Now that worship has begun, do the following:

Start on time. If worship begins at 11:00 A.M., that is when the service should start.

Pick up the pace of worship. Eliminate all dead spots. Remember how irritating those little pauses are between television shows? Do not irritate the congregation with unintentional stops and pauses. Listen to an audiotape of the service and time the amount of dead sound in the service. Eliminate every unintentional silent spot.

Shorten the prayers led by worship leaders. Longer prayers often are unfocused or repetitious. Encourage laity to lead corporate prayer. Teach people how to pray and let them pray. Use bidding prayers—specific prayer requests followed by a time of silence. For variety, offer not only traditional collects but try Tongsung Kido, a Korean prayer when a congregation is given a specific time period and a common petition, and then everyone prays aloud for that petition at the same time.

Use more music. Make a service of worship at least 40 percent music (twenty-four minutes of an hour-long service). When music is less than 40 percent of a service, a congregation is probably stable in membership or declining. Remember that every act of worship, from the Greeting to the Benediction, may be sung by a choir, a soloist, or a congregation. The more music the better.

Pick singable hymns and choruses. Take a song/hymn survey of the congregation and use at least one beloved song in every service. Add a contemporary Christian chorus as a call to worship, or to precede an opening hymn, or as a response to the Word, or as a congregational benediction. The blending of music is the heart of a Blended service.

When you use new songs and hymns, provide an opportunity for the congregation to learn the words and music they will sing in worship. Good singing involves, at the least, firm vocal leadership from either a choir or a song leader (with a nice voice rather than waving hands), strong instrumental support, and a clear pattern of teaching new music to a congregation. Use the bulletin, if there is one, to explain why the song or hymn is being used; then enthusiastically teach the words and music.

Use a variety of instruments. In addition to pianos and organs, use guitars, drums, and synthesizers. Every congregation has a host of instrumentalists who may be used weekly, once a month, or for seasonal celebrations. Do not save brass players for Easter Sunday only.

Involve children. Worship is for adults, youth, and children. If the children are engaged, so are the adults. Encourage children to read Scripture, take up the offering, dance, sing, and lead in prayer.

Use the lectionary. The lectionary provides a basic, systematic introduction to Scripture and the gospel's narrative for all of God's people. Typically, use only one of the three lessons of the day (the Gospel lesson on the Sundays from Advent to Pentecost and any one of the three lessons in Ordinary Time after Pentecost).

Get rid of manuscripts for preaching. Everyone should be able to see the preacher's eyes throughout the service and especially the sermon. Write out or carefully outline sermons to gain clarity of focus and intent, and then put the text away.

Preach in the midst of a congregation. Come out from behind the pulpit and move among the listeners.

Make the preaching relevant. Preaching should be more biblical than doctrinal, more concrete than abstract, more relational than detached, more imaginative and visual than didactic, more oral than written. Tell concrete Bible stories, use real-life examples, avoid theological jargon, use "I" rather than "we," avoid thematic outlines, and write for the ear and not the eye.

Ask, "Who will care?" about the theme of the sermon. Does the sermon actually address a real concern of any particular individual or any particular audience within a congregation? If the preacher cannot specifically name "who cares," the sermon should be recrafted.

Invite positive, specific, and concrete prayer responses to the Word. Prayer may be spoken or silent, led by laity or clergy. Encourage the use of the prayer rail and human touch and provide opportunities for the congregation to come forward.

Use the gifts of a congregation. Ask dancers, actors, and visual artists to share their gifts. Encourage participants to involve their whole bodies, their dramatic talents, drawing, painting, sewing, and other skills in worship.

Provide more visuals. Can a person with impaired hearing enjoy worship? Use banners, slides, video clips, decorations, and other objects that help everyone know what is going on in worship.

Make the sacraments visible. Move the communion table front and center. Pastors should stand behind the table so the taking, blessing, breaking, and giving are clearly visible. During baptisms, move the baptismal font front and center. Ask family and friends of the candidates to stand behind the pastor. Make the washing visible. When adults come for baptism as a sign of their first commitment to the gospel, focus the service on that adult conversion and subsequent commitments.

Use newer liturgies such as healing services or baptismal reaffirmations that involve the whole congregation. Allow people the opportunity to be touched for healing or to touch water and remember their baptism.

Make financial offerings specific and for concrete needs. Designated giving is replacing unified budgets. Write this announcement each Sunday: "Visitors are invited not to contribute during the offering because you are our guests." Such an announcement does not denigrate the offering but makes clear that believers and members are expected to give and that seekers are invited to participate at whatever level they feel comfortable. Too many congregations welcome guests primarily because the congregations need financial help. Experience has shown that such an announcement increases giving from both members and guests.

Remember that few people will respond to verbal invitations to join a congregation. Calls for commitments must be short and specific, such as an invitation to join a one-week mission work team. Invitations to church membership will be among the last commitments the new generations will make. Most decisions to join a congregation are now made in a small group or in the pastor's office. Seekers and new hearers must be carefully nurtured toward membership.

End on time. Or better yet, end a worship service five minutes early. Do not run over unless the extra time is absolutely necessary.

Finally, evaluate every service with the worship team and congregation. Use a worship team to be the ears in a congregation. Ask weekly: What worked well, what was learned, what can be improved?

Every worship team and congregation must decide how to shape its worship. Will we begin a new service? Will we begin to blend worship together? Will we stay where we are? Never, however, make such decisions without remembering these primary questions:

What gospel do we proclaim?
Which people need this gospel?

A PARABLE

Soon after the creation of the United States of America, John Wesley made a secret journey to the new land. He wanted to see how well the circuit riders, guided by Francis Asbury, the new bishop, were sharing the gospel on the American frontier. Mr. Wesley landed in Wilmington, North Carolina, and made his way west. One Sunday, Mr. Wesley came to a small settlement near the Yadkin River where he heard a young circuit rider had gathered a society of new believers.

When Mr. Wesley came into the village, he heard no sounds. All the houses were empty. Even the Methodist meetinghouse, the home of a lay leader, had no occupants. Mr. Wesley became worried. Had the people been seized and dragged from the town? Had a plague destroyed the village? He knew that on Sunday good Methodists would be in their meetinghouse singing Charles Wesley's hymns, following the lectionary, reading the liturgy of the Word, and celebrating the Lord's Supper using the *Sunday Service for the People Called Methodist* that he had adapted from the *Book of Common Prayer* in 1784. Where were all the Methodists?

Then, in the distance, Mr. Wesley heard some singing. He did not recognize the tune, but he followed the sound.

Down by the river, Mr. Wesley discovered the whole village. Women, men, and children were gathered around the young circuit rider, who was standing on a tree stump, singing spiritual songs that came from African slaves. The circuit rider then opened a Bible and read a text other than that assigned by the lectionary.

Mr. Wesley was livid. The veins in his neck stood out. His face turned red. He pushed his way through the crowd up to the circuit rider. Even before the circuit rider could begin to preach, Mr. Wesley asked the young man if he knew who he was. The circuit rider replied, "Of course, Mr. Wesley, I would recognize your face anywhere." Then Mr. Wesley demanded an explanation. Why were the Methodists not in their meetinghouse, singing Charles's songs, following the lectionary, reading the liturgy, and celebrating the Lord's Supper? Mr. Wesley had written down exactly how Methodists were to worship in the new world. Singing African spirituals outdoors and reading alternative passages from Scripture was not worship!

The young circuit rider jumped off his stump and asked Mr. Wesley to sit down before he had a heart attack. It would not do for Mr. Wesley to die in the American wilderness. As Mr. Wesley sat, the circuit rider told him a story.

Once upon a time, a farmer was riding his horse-drawn wagon to market. Although he and his horse followed the same road every week, the farmer held the horse's reins tightly in his hands. When the road turned left, the farmer jerked hard on the reins pulling the horse's head to the left. When the road turned right, the farmer pulled the reins hard to the right, cutting the bit into the horse's mouth. Although the farmer and his horse always got to market, the horse was always exhausted and bleeding at the mouth.

One day, the farmer passed a traveler on the road. The sojourner saw how the farmer manipulated and abused the horse. The traveler cried out to the farmer: "Let go the reins." On a whim, the farmer let go of the reins. He believed that the horse would stop, become lost, and waste their time. How could the horse know what to do without the farmer's firm hand?

Then an amazing thing happened. The horse turned, looked at the farmer, and began to walk ahead slowly, staying precisely in the middle of the road. As the journey continued, the horse began to move more quickly, still never leaving the narrow path. By the time the horse and driver reached the town, the horse had begun to dance. They arrived in town more quickly than ever before. The horse was free and fresh. Letting go of the reins changed forever the relationship between the farmer and his horse, as well as their ability to accomplish their common task.

As he finished the story, the circuit rider replied, "Mr. Wesley, we love your *Sunday Service,* but it just won't work in this new world. Mr. Wesley, let go the reins."

Mr. Wesley returned to England, never again to return to the United States. And he wondered, until his dying day, what God and he had created.

In our worship, let go the reins. Let God and the people lead our worship. And when we all arrive together in God's new millennium, we will be freer and fresher and richer for the experience.

CONTEMPORARY WORSHIP PATTERNS

LITURGICAL	PRAISE AND WORSHIP	SEEKER
DEFINITION:		
formal	informal	choreographed
lectionary	topical	contemporary issues
textual	oral	aural and visual
sacramental	musical	presentational
hymnal	praise chorus book	sheet music
historic continuity	contemporary life	cultural relevance
cerebral	emotional	informational
focus on ear	focus on heart	focus on eye
old mainline	new mainline	independent
AUDIENCE:		
churched believers	churched believers	unchurched seekers
churched seekers	churched seekers	singles
unconnected believers	unconnected believers	unconnected believers
builders/boomers	boomers/busters	boomers/busters/ millennials

LITURGICAL	PRAISE AND WORSHIP	SEEKER

PRIMARY THEOLOGICAL CONCERN:

LITURGICAL	PRAISE AND WORSHIP	SEEKER
sin	brokenness	ignorance

EVANGELISTIC TASK:

LITURGICAL	PRAISE AND WORSHIP	SEEKER
house for believers	porch for hearers	steps for seekers
sanctifying grace	justifying grace	prevenient grace
advanced catechesis	introductory catechesis	precatechesis

SOURCES:

LITURGICAL	PRAISE AND WORSHIP	SEEKER
hymnals & prayer-books	radio	television
tradition	experience	reason

ROLE OF CONGREGATION:

LITURGICAL	PRAISE AND WORSHIP	SEEKER
participants	participants	passive audience
liturgists	choir	observers

SETTING AND ENVIRONMENT:

LITURGICAL	PRAISE AND WORSHIP	SEEKER
sanctuary	auditorium	theater
pulpit	lectern	stool
font	pool	screen
altar/table	table	stage
pews	chairs	theater seating
Sunday A.M.	Sunday or Wednesday P.M.	Saturday, Thursday, or Sunday P.M.
worship bulletin	announcement sheet	announcement sheet

LITURGICAL	PRAISE AND WORSHIP	SEEKER
SHAPE OF SERVICE:		
Entrance	Worship	Thematic Performance
Proclamation & Response	Teaching	Question & Answer
Thanksgiving with Holy Communion		
Sending Forth		
LEADERS:		
pastor	teacher	speaker
choir director	worship leader	band leader
organist	pianist to orchestra	band, drama team
some volunteers	many volunteers	professionals
MUSIC:		
"Joyful, Joyful" (UMH #89)	"El Shaddai" (UMH #123)	"Come Sunday" (UMH #728)
communal	individual	listened to
hymns	choruses/hymns	popular music
choir & congregation	leader & congregation	leaders only
organ & piano	keyboard	percussion & tape
hymnal	chorus books	video projector
low to high cost	low to high cost	high cost
TECHNOLOGY:		
low to high	medium to high	medium to high

low: line out hymns, no bulletin, a cappella singing, piano

LITURGICAL	PRAISE AND WORSHIP	SEEKER

medium: overhead projector, slide projector, synthesizer with
   speakers
high: video/data projector, karaoke, CD with graphics display

PREACHING:

lectionary based	continuous readings	thematic
exegetical	expository	explanatory
eucharistic	kerygmatic	didactic
pastor as presider	pastor as teacher	pastor as guide
transparent style	personality	personality

VARIABLES:

degree of formality	length of singing	dress code
textual or oral	planned spontaneity	financial offering
role of choir	songbooks	video clips
invitation to join	musical instruments	
frequency of communion		

ISSUES/PROBLEMS:

tyranny of tradition	tyranny of experience	tyranny of culture
fear of change	fear of tradition	fear of stagnation
lack of style	lack of content	lack of depth
believers only	hearers only	seekers only
too pessimistic	too optimistic	too educational
too formal	too informal	too choreographed
participation	performance	entertainment
too textual	lack of musical integrity	lack of participation

LITURGICAL	PRAISE AND WORSHIP	SEEKER
ignorance of new styles	ignorance of tradition	worship as commodity
culturally irrelevant	culturally bound	not "worship"
creates dependence	creates dependence	creates dependence
otherworldly	materialistic	too focused on needs
needs small groups	needs small groups	needs small groups

WORSHIP STYLES

PARTICIPATION	PERFORMANCE	ENTERTAINMENT
Tradition driven	*Aesthetic/enlighten-ment driven*	*Culture driven*
1. Celebration (liturgical, African American, Quaker)	1. Self-expression (traditional Protestant worship)	1. Connection with seekers (alternative seeker)
2. People's praise and prayer	2. Leader's performance	2. Technology's effect (screen and media's power)
3. Values participation	3. Values performance	3. Values contemporary expression
4. Leaders preside and prompt	4. Leaders perform	4. Leaders entertain
5. Performance enhances and	5. Performance tends to call	5. Performance evokes a

PARTICIPATION	PERFORMANCE	ENTERTAINMENT
Tradition driven	*Aesthetic/enlighten-* *ment driven*	*Culture* *driven*
prompts participation	attention to itself (applause)	hearing/ attention
6. Focuses on living water (mystery)	6. Focuses on the bucket	6. Focuses on living water (anti-mystery)
7. Arts embody the Word	7. Arts express underlying autonomy of performers	7. Arts prepare hearers for the Word
8. Music as corporate expression	8. Music as mix of corporate and leaders' expression	8. Music as entertainment
9. The gospel enacted and delighted in	9. The gospel understood	9. The gospel considered/ heard
10. Consciousness and life transformed	10. Awareness heightened	10. First hearing
11. Danger: partic- ipation without relevance; failure to connect with the daily life	11. Danger: content without partic- ipation that builds vital faith	11. Danger: relevance without content or participation
12. God is object and subject	12. God is the object through	12. God is the object through

Appendix 2

PARTICIPATION	PERFORMANCE	ENTERTAINMENT
Tradition driven	*Aesthetic/enlighten-ment driven*	*Culture driven*
through Word and sacraments	tradition and forms	contemporary idioms and media
13. Image: an enclosed garden	13. Image: art museum in midsize city	13. Image: post-modern high rise made of mirrored glass

APPENDIX 3

STRUCTURES OF A CONGREGATION'S EVANGELISTIC TASK

"Go therefore and make disciples of all nations, baptizing them in the name of the Father and of the Son and of the Holy Spirit, and teaching them to obey everything that I have commanded you." Matthew 28:19-20

STEPS (hearing)	PORCH (testing and deciding)	INITIATION (baptism)	HOUSE (ministry in daily life)
	PRECATECHESIS	**CATECHESIS**	
Task	*Preconversion*	*Conversion*	*Continuing conversion*
	Listening to people interpreting the gospel	*Forming persons for living the gospel*	
Strategy	*Researching, interpreting and reaching the culture*	*Learning and celebrating the Christian tradition for ministry in daily life*	
Audience	*Seekers*	*Hearers*	*Believers*

Appendix 3

	PORCH	**INITIATION**	**HOUSE**
Aim	*First hearing*	*Conversion*	*Full participation*
God's Action	*Prevenient grace*	*Justifying grace*	*Sanctifying grace*
Mode	*Presentation*	*Instruction*	*Participation*
Settings	*Preworship* ⇨*seeker services* ⇨*observer in public worship* ⇨*small group*	*Transforming worship & small groups for formation of disciples*	*& small groups for continuing support of disciples*

CHRISTIAN INITIATION AS A PRECONVERSION/ CONVERSION JOURNEY

Stages

Inquiry ↓ Hearing ↓ Candidacy ↓ Integration ⟶

Services

Welcome   Calling to baptism   Baptism

"Adult baptism is the norm when the Church is in a missionary situation, reaching out to persons in a culture which is indifferent or hostile to the faith. While the baptism of infants is appropriate for Christian families, the increasingly minority status of the Church in contemporary society demands more attention to evangelizing, nurturing, and baptizing adult converts."

(*By Water and Spirit: A United Methodist Understanding of Baptism*, p. 13)

NOTES

Introduction

1. Advertisement from Belmont United Methodist Church in Nashville, Tennessee, 1991.

2. Annie Dillard, *Teaching a Stone to Talk* (New York: Harper and Row, 1982), 40.

1. Three Patterns of Contemporary Worship

1. See James White's *Protestant Worship: Traditions in Transition* (Louisville: Westminster/John Knox, 1989) for an excellent discussion of changing worship in the Lutheran, Reformed, Methodist, and Pentecostal traditions, among others. Also see White's *Introduction to Christian Worship*, rev. ed. (Nashville: Abingdon, 1990), chapter 1, for a discussion of global liturgical options.

2. James White, *Protestant Worship*, 209.

3. Ibid., 212.

4. Dan Benedict and Craig Miller, *Contemporary Worship for the Twenty-First Century* (Nashville, Discipleship Resources, 1994), is the best source that describes and critiques these three styles of worship.

5. The categories of Participation—Performance—Entertainment are best described by Dan Benedict in appendix 2. Another option describes Presentational worship versus Participatory worship, as found in Net Fax Number 54 (September 16, 1996) by Leadership Network.

6. See appendix 3 for a description of the structures of the church's evangelistic task as it relates to the three styles of worship.

7. See Dan Benedict, *Come to the Waters: Baptism and Our Ministry of Welcoming Seekers and Making Disciples* (Nashville: Discipleship Resources, 1996) for the United Methodist model of adult incorporation.

8. Charles Trueheart has an excellent description of these new communities in "Welcome to the Next Church," *Atlantic*, August 1996, 37-58.

9. See *Abingdon/Cokesbury Chorus Book I* (Nashville: Abingdon, 1996) by Andy Langford et al. for one collection of popular contemporary Christian music. This

collection enables Liturgical churches to integrate contemporary music into more traditional liturgies. Further volumes in this series are planned for future years.

10. The debate becomes most focused in Marva Dawn's *Reaching Out Without Dumbing Down* (Grand Rapids: Eerdmans, 1995), which criticizes these services as appealing to the lowest common denominator, and, in contrast, Sally Morgenthaler's *Worship Evangelism* (Grand Rapids: Zondervan, 1995), which sees their value in reaching new people for Jesus Christ.

11. George Hunter, *Church for the Unchurched* (Nashville: Abingdon, 1996), 71.

12. Rick Warren, "Worship Can Be a Witness," *Worship Leader* 6 (January-February 1997), 28.

2. Origins of Contemporary Worship

1. *The United Methodist Hymnal: Book of United Methodist Worship* (Nashville: United Methodist Publishing House, 1989) also has a number of supplemental volumes of music and commentaries. *The United Methodist Book of Worship* (Nashville: United Methodist Publishing House, 1992) has an Accompaniment Edition plus commentaries.

For a full discussion of and practical ways to use *The United Methodist Hymnal* and *The United Methodist Book of Worship*, see the following Abingdon publications: *The Worship Resources of The United Methodist Hymnal*, Hoyt L. Hickman, volume editor, 1989; *The Hymns of The United Methodist Hymnal*, Diana Sanchez, volume editor, 1989; *Blueprints for Worship: A User's Guide for United Methodist Congregations*, Andy Langford, 1993; and *Companion to The United Methodist Hymnal*, Carlton R. Young, 1993.

2. *Mil Voces Para Celebrar: Himnario Metodista* (Nashville: United Methodist Publishing House, 1996) is the official Spanish-language hymnal of The United Methodist Church. While much of its liturgy is based on English-language texts, it and all other hymnals and books of worship in other languages have particular cultural adaptations.

3. For examples of this occurrence in other denominations, see the 1978 *Lutheran Book of Worship*, the 1985 *Book of Alternative Services* of the Anglican Church of Canada, the 1986 *Book of Worship of the United Church of Christ*, the 1987 *Thankful Praise* of the Disciples of Christ, and the Presbyterian Church (U.S.A.) and Cumberland Presbyterian Church 1993 *Book of Common Worship*, which all reflect similar decisions.

4. See Frank C. Senn, " 'Worship Alive': An Analysis and Critique of 'Alternative Worship Services,' " *Worship* 69 (May 1995): 194-224, for a strong negative critique of effervescent worship from a Lutheran perspective. The difficulty with Senn's analysis is that he makes no differentiation between any of the alternative services.

5. Charles G. Finney, *Lectures on the Revivals of Religion* (1835; reprint, ed. William G. McLoughlin, Cambridge, Mass.: Belknap, 1960).

6. James White, *Protestant Worship: Traditions in Transition* (Louisville: Westminster/John Knox, 1989), 210.

3. Generational Culture Wars

1. Craig Miller, *Baby Boomer Spirituality* (Nashville: Discipleship Resources, 1992) is an excellent introduction to this generation and its relationship with God.

Lee Strobel of Willow Creek in *Inside the Mind of Unchurched Harry and Mary* (Grand Rapids: Zondervan, 1993) also describes their relationship with the church. Tim Wright in *A Community of Joy* (Nashville: Abingdon, 1994) has insights into this particular generation and the implications for worship. Other valuable books include *Vanishing Boundaries* by Dean Hoge et al. (Louisville: Westminster/John Knox, 1994) and Wade Clark Roof's *A Generation of Seekers* (San Francisco: Harper, 1994).

2. Books describing the busters' generation include Craig Miller's *Post Moderns: The Beliefs, Hopes, and Fears of Young Americans* (Nashville: Discipleship Resources, 1997); George Barna's *Baby Busters: Disillusioned Generation* (Chicago: Northfield, 1994); Tim Celek and Dieter Zander's *Inside the Soul of the Next Generation* (Grand Rapids: Zondervan, 1996); and Bill Strauss and Neil Howe's *Thirteenth Gen: Abort, Retry, Ignore, Fail?* (New York: Random, 1993).

3. George Hunter, *Church for the Unchurched* (Nashville: Abingdon, 1996), 24, and throughout this seminal book. Hunter describes these new generations as pre-Christian in an attempt to understand these generations as a mission field.

4. From notes from May 1995 seminar on contemporary worship at Lake Junaluska, North Carolina. Webber is one of the best interpreters of Liturgical worship for Praise and Worship leaders and Blended worship for Liturgical congregations. See his latest book, *Planning Blended Worship: The Creative Mixture of Old and New* (Nashville: Abingdon, 1998).

5. Wade Clark Roof, "The Changing American Religious Landscape and Implications for Ritual," paper at a meeting of the North American Academy of Liturgy in January 1994. See also his book, *A Generation of Seekers*.

6. See Wright's book *A Community of Joy: How to Create Contemporary Worship* (Nashville, Abingdon, 1994).

7. From an interview with Martin Marty as reported in "Historian Blends Intellect, Curiosity, Stamina," *Charlotte Observer*, January 21, 1995, page 5c.

8. Gregor Goethals, *The TV Ritual: Worship at the Video Altar* (Boston: Beacon, 1981), 143-44, as quoted in Susan White, *Christian Worship and Technological Change* (Nashville: Abingdon, 1994), 125.

4. Worship as a Means of Grace

1. Quotations from 1919 newspaper commentary on the painting *The Wyandot Indian Mission* as found on a lithograph on the painting.

2. For a full copy and discussion of Wesley's liturgy for the North American Methodists, see *John Wesley's Prayer Book: The Sunday Service of the Methodists in North America*, ed. James F. White (Cleveland: OSL Publications, 1991). *The Sunday Service* was Wesley's own revision of *The Book of Common Prayer* of the Church of England particularly for a new people in a new country with a new culture and new needs.

3. *The Works of John Wesley*, ed. Thomas Jackson (1831; reprint, Grand Rapids: Zondervan, 1959), 5:187-88. Wesley defines five instituted means of grace—the Word of God, Holy Communion, prayer, Christian conference, and fasts. I have expanded Holy Communion to include Baptism. In Wesley's day, most persons were baptized as infants and adult baptism exceptionally rare. Wesley's sermon "On Baptism" however, makes clear that Baptism is a sure means of grace. Christian conference, a complex term in Wesley's theology, is described in this book as

fellowship. Because of its more personal and private nature, fasting is not included in this discussion.

4. *The Letters of John Wesley*, ed. John Telford (London: Epworth, 1931), 3:366-67.

5. Adrian Burdon, " 'Till in Heaven . . .'—Wesleyan Models for Liturgical Theology" in *Worship* 71 (1997): 313. This article describes various aspects of John Wesley's liturgical thought.

6. See Thomas A. Langford's *Practical Divinity: Theology in the Wesleyan Tradition*, rev. ed., 2 vols. (Nashville: Abingdon, 1998–99) for an introduction to John Wesley's theology and that of his religious heirs.

7. See Thomas A. Langford III, "The Means of Grace: Worship in the Wesleyan Tradition" (Master's thesis, Emory University, 1982) and other writings on this topic, especially *Blueprints for Worship* (Nashville: Abingdon, 1993), for an attempt to relate Wesley's understanding of the means of grace to current church life.

8. The primary source of the disagreement between the Arminians (Wesleyans) and Calvinists lies in their different understandings of human nature. Both Calvinists and Wesleyans agree on doctrines of original sin, the free grace of God, justification by faith, and the centrality of Scripture. Both affirm that worship is God's self-communication with humanity toward the end that people are changed in word and deed. What is significantly different is the role of the human response in God's work of salvation. Because of the Fall, Calvinists deny the possibility of free human response. God alone saves. Whether people hear the Word is ultimately God's activity. Functionally, Calvinists preach Christ and then let God do the work to save the elect, those who are foreordained by God for salvation. Because of this perspective, John Calvin spent most of his career in Geneva preaching to the same gathering of people in the same community and wrote extended commentaries on successive books of the Bible. All of this was a trusting affirmation of God's sovereignty.

Geoffrey Wainwright on Wesley and Calvin: Sources for Theology, Liturgy, and Spirituality (Australia: Joint Board of Christian Education of Australia and New Zealand, 1989) is a thorough discussion of the differences between these two schools of thought and implications of them for worship.

9. See David Luecke, *The Other Story of Lutherans at Worship: Reclaiming Our Heritage of Diversity* (Tempe, Ariz.: Fellowship Ministries, 1995) for a passionate defense of Lutherans worshiping in a contemporary style as opposed to worshiping only through the *Lutheran Book of Worship*.

10. *Book of Concord*, trans. and ed. Theodore G. Tappert (Philadelphia: Muhlenberg Press, 1959), 612.

11. Article 15 of the Articles of Religion as found in *John Wesley's Prayer Book*, ed. James White, 311.

12. Susan White, *Christian Worship and Technological Change* (Nashville: Abingdon, 1994), 128, quoting Raymond Fosdick, "The Atomic Age and the Good Life" from *Within Our Power: Perspectives for a Time of Peril* (New York: Longman's, 1952), 70.

5. Enriching Worship: First Steps First

1. The church has always understood that worship reflects belief. The classic formulation of this understanding is from Prosper of Aquitaine in the fifth century, "*Ut legem credendi, lex statuat supplicandi*," which is often shortened to read

"lex orandi, lex credendi"—what we pray is what we believe. This concept implies that everything the community does in worship reflects what the community truly believes.

2. D. T. Niles, "Venite Adoremus II," in *World's Student Christian Federation Prayer Book* (1938), 105-6.

6. Four Cornerstones

1. *The Revised Common Lectionary* (Nashville: Abingdon, 1992) contains the full calendar and readings for the Christian year, along with introductory commentary. "The Revised Common Lectionary 1992: A Revision for the Next Generation" by Andy Langford in *Quarterly Review* 13 (Summer 1993): 37-48 provides an overview of the lectionary.

2. See *By Water and the Spirit: Making Connections for Identity and Ministry* by Gayle Carlton Felton (Nashville: Discipleship Resources, 1997) for the official United Methodist view of baptism and its implications. This is the first time United Methodists have clearly stated their sacramental and evangelical theology of baptism.

7. New Services and Blended Worship

1. Ed Dobson, *Starting a Seeker-Sensitive Service* (Grand Rapids: Zondervan, 1993) is the best book available on starting new services. He describes the joys, costs, and hurts of starting a new service for new people. Elmer Towns, *How to Go to Two Services* (Forest, Va.: Church Growth Institute) is a video presentation on this topic.

2. This Blended model is seen in a number of growing mainline congregations such as Frazier Memorial United Methodist Church in Montgomery, Alabama. This service, seen widely on television, may be termed a seeker-friendly preaching service.

3. Michael Slaughter at Ginghamsburg United Methodist Church outside of Dayton, Ohio, has a high-tech Praise and Worship service that is seeker-sensitive. The sanctuary is centered on a video screen, with half a dozen musical synthesizers and other instruments leading worship. The members at Ginghamsburg, however, have begun to use hymns again in their four Praise and Worship services.

ANNOTATED BIBLIOGRAPHY

Barna, George. *Baby Busters: Disillusioned Generation.* Chicago: Northfield Publishing, 1994. Barna's research details the lives and values of the busters, and implications for congregations in outreach to and worshiping with this new generation.

———. *The Frog in the Kettle: What Christians Need to Know about Life in the Year Two Thousand.* Ventura, Calif.: Regal, 1990. Predicting a fragmented society, Barna offers ways to reconsider ministry in the new millennium with new generations.

Benedict, Dan. *Come to the Waters: Baptism and Our Ministry of Welcoming Seekers and Making Disciples.* Nashville: Discipleship Resources, 1996. Prepares United Methodists to incorporate new persons into the church through an intensive period of preparation. First in the Christian Initiation Series.

Benedict, Dan, and Craig Miller. *Contemporary Worship for the Twenty-First Century: Worship or Evangelism?* Nashville: Discipleship Resources, 1994. A landmark book describing three patterns of contemporary worship, with examples and evaluations of these specific worship styles.

Carson, Tim, and Kathy Carson. *So You're Thinking About Contemporary Worship.* St. Louis: Chalice Press, 1997. A practical guide by local church leaders out of the Christian Church tradition.

Celek, Tim, and Dieter Zander, *Inside the Soul of the Next Genera-*

tion: Insights and Strategies for Reaching Busters. Grand Rapids: Zondervan, 1996. Insights and strategies for the church to reach the baby busters.

Christian Century 114 (May 14, 1997): 479-85 has three articles on Seeker services, their leaders, congregations, and books.

Church Growth Institute, P.O. Box 7000, Waterlick Road, Forest, VA 24551-9970 offers books and other resources in a conservative, evangelical approach seeking new generations.

Dawn, Marva J. *Reaching Out Without Dumbing Down: A Theology of Worship for the Turn-of-the-Century Culture.* Grand Rapids: Eerdmans, 1995. Stridently encourages worship leaders to resist worship changes in order to be faithful to the gospel.

Dobson, Ed. *Starting a Seeker-Sensitive Service.* Grand Rapids: Zondervan, 1993. A conservative pastor details how his congregation began a Seeker service, with many helpful suggestions and warnings.

Dyer, Scott, and Nancy Beach. *The Source: A Resource Guide for Using Creative Arts in Church Services.* Grand Rapids: Zondervan, 1996. A wonderful sourcebook that includes video and musical suggestions to interpret to seekers life issues and Christian responses.

Easum, William M. *Worship in the 1990's.* Port Aransas, Tex.: Twenty-First Century Strategies, 1992. An outline and overview of the context for contemporary worship.

Fagerberg, David W. "Was the Cathedral of Notre Dame a Megachurch?" in *Pro Ecclesia* 6 (Spring 1997): 41-47. This short article compares a liturgical church that is ritualized, hierarchical, sacred, sacramental, traditional, and iconic with alternative services that are none of the above.

Felton, Gayle Carlton. *By Water and the Spirit: Making Connections for Identity and Ministry.* Nashville: Discipleship Resources, 1997. Introduction to the new United Methodist baptismal statement and its implications for church life.

Graham, Kevin, and Kevin G. Ford. *Jesus for a New Generation: Putting the Gospel in the Language of Xers.* Downers Grove, Ill.:

InterVarsity, 1995. A helpful book about Generation X and what religious strategies work with them.

Hoge, Dean; Benton Johnson; and Donald Luidens. *Vanishing Boundaries: The Religion of Mainline Protestant Baby Boomers.* Louisville: Westminster/John Knox, 1994. An in-depth survey of baby boomers and the surprising implications of their faith journey for mainline congregations.

Hunter, George. *Church for the Unchurched.* Nashville: Abingdon, 1996. Hunter's analysis of postmodern society, successful congregations in several denominations, and the opportunity for a new apostolic age for the church.

———. *How to Reach Secular People.* Nashville: Abingdon, 1992. A United Methodist teacher describes how to engage secular persons, primarily boomers.

Hybels, Lynne, and Bill Hybels. *Rediscovering Church: The Story and Vision of Willow Creek Community Church.* Grand Rapids: Zondervan, 1995. The founding couple of Willow Creek describes why and how they created the church that began Seeker services.

Kallestad, Walt. *Entertainment Evangelism: Taking the Church Public.* Nashville: Abingdon, 1996. The senior pastor of the Lutheran Community Church of Joy in Phoenix integrates worship with evangelism.

Kenneson, Philip. "Selling [Out] the Church in the Marketplace of Desire." *Modern Theology* 9 (October 1993): 319-48. A serious critique of worship that uses market forces as the primary authorities of truth.

Kenneson, Philip, and James L. Street. *Selling Out the Church: The Dangers of Church Marketing.* Nashville: Abingdon, 1997. Responding to church marketing, reminds the church that the gospel is not for exchange or sale.

Langford, Andy. *Blueprints for Worship: A User's Guide for United Methodist Congregations.* Nashville: Abingdon, 1993. The companion to *The United Methodist Book of Worship* (Nashville: Abingdon, 1992), with suggestions on how to use Liturgical worship services more effectively.

Langford, Andy, and Sally Langford. *Worship and Evangelism.* Nashville: Discipleship Resources, 1989. Out of print. A description of why and how worship and evangelism are part of the same task, with an emphasis on making Liturgical worship more seeker-friendly.

Langford, Andy, et al. *Abingdon/Cokesbury Chorus Book I.* Nashville: Abingdon, 1996. A collection of popular contemporary choruses for mainline churches. The collection is organized by the Word and Table pattern of worship, with inclusive language, global songs, and extensive indexes.

Luecke, David S. *The Other Story of Lutherans at Worship: Reclaiming Our Heritage of Diversity.* Tempe, Ariz.: Fellowship Ministries, 1995. Presents alternative Lutheran worship practices from historical, theological, and practical perspectives.

McDonald, William P. *Gracious Voices: Shouts and Whispers for God Seekers.* Nashville: Discipleship Resources, 1997. A sourcebook of prayers and readings to lead seekers through inquiry, welcome, formation, calling to baptism, and baptism. Part of the Christian Initiation Series by Discipleship Resources.

Miller, Craig. *Baby Boomer Spirituality: Ten Essential Values of a Generation.* Nashville: Discipleship Resources, 1992. An excellent introduction to the culture and religious views of the boomers.

————. *Post Moderns: The Beliefs, Hopes, and Fears of Young Americans.* Nashville: Discipleship Resources, 1997. Describes baby busters and how the church may reach them, from a nontraditional United Methodist perspective.

Morgenthaler, Sally. *Worship Evangelism: Inviting Unbelievers into the Presence of God.* Grand Rapids: Zondervan, 1995. A book of the year that addresses the issues of worship and evangelism and the converting power of liturgy.

Pritchard, Gregory A. *Willow Creek Seeker Services: Evaluating a New Way of Doing Church.* Grand Rapids: Baker, 1995. A review of the early years of Willow Creek, followed by a critique. The material is dated, but the critique identifies major concerns by outsiders of Seeker services.

Roof, Wade Clark. "The Changing American Religious Landscape and Implications for Ritual." North American Academy of Liturgy Proceedings, January 1994. A sociologist reviews changes in American culture and how these changes affect worship.

―――――. *A Generation of Seekers: The Spiritual Journeys of the Baby Boom Generation.* San Francisco: Harper, 1994. A landmark study of the beliefs of the baby boomers.

Schowalter, Richard P. *Igniting a New Generation of Believers.* Nashville: Abingdon, 1995. How to reach baby boomers by focusing on particular needs of this generation. One chapter is on worship: "A Golden Key or a Rusty Door?"

Senn, Frank. " 'Worship Alive': An Analysis and Critique of 'Alternative Worship Services.' " in *Worship* 69 (May 1995): 194-224. Strong negative critique of contemporary worship from a distinctly Lutheran perspective.

Slaughter, Michael. *Spiritual Entrepreneurs: Six Principles for Risking Renewal.* Nashville: Abingdon, 1995. A United Methodist pastor describes how he transformed a traditional small church into a major congregation, with a special emphasis on the role of worship.

Strauss, Bill, and Neil Howe. *Thirteenth Gen: Abort, Retry, Ignore, Fail?* New York: Random, 1993. How to understand and reach the baby busters.

Strobel, Lee. *Inside the Mind of Unchurched Harry and Mary: Why People Steer Clear of God and the Church and How You Can Respond.* Grand Rapids: Zondervan, 1993. The teaching pastor of Willow Creek describes the attitudes of unchurched seekers and how to reach them.

Townley, Cathy. *Come Celebrate: A Guide for Planning Contemporary Worship* (with Mike Graham) and *Come Celebrate: Songbooks.* Nashville: Abingdon, 1995 and following. The Guide is a step-by-step workbook for worship teams creating new worship styles, while the songbooks break new ground in contemporary choruses.

Trueheart, Charles. "Welcome to the Next Church." *Atlantic.* (August 1996): 37-58. A layperson's journey among the megachurches, with a focus on their worship and the new communities they are creating.

Webber, Robert. *Blended Worship: Achieving Substance and Relevance in Worship.* Peabody, Mass.: Hendrickson, 1996. Examines a variety of worship styles and the ways in which these may be practiced in churches today.

————. *Planning Blended Worship: The Creative Mixture of Old and New.* Nashville: Abingdon, 1998. An introduction to blending Liturgical, Praise and Worship, and Seeker services.

Wenz, Robert. *Room for God? A Worship Challenge for a Church-Growth and Marketing Era.* Grand Rapids: Baker, 1994. encourages churches not to sell out the gospel in seeking to meet the needs of people in our culture.

White, James. *Protestant Worship: Traditions in Transition.* Louisville: Westminster/John Knox, 1989. An overview of nine Protestant liturgical traditions and their futures.

White, Susan. *Christian Worship and Technological Change.* Nashville: Abingdon, 1994. A professional liturgist demonstrates how changes in technology through the ages have affected worship, along with the implications of changes anticipated due to the technological revolution.

The World Wide Web has thousands of sites, of persons, congregations, and organizations addressing contemporary worship. Use a search engine and begin surfing.

Worship Leader. A bi-monthly magazine for leaders most interested in the cutting edge of Praise and Worship and Seeker services. 107 Kenner Ave., Nashville, TN 37205.

Wright, Tim. *A Community of Joy: How to Create Contemporary Worship.* Nashville: Abingdon, 1994. A basic introduction to contemporary worship by a Lutheran leader.

————. *Unfinished Evangelism: More Than Getting Them in the Door.* Philadelphia: Augsburg Fortress, 1995. How congregations with Seeker services need to move persons into discipleship.

Wright, Tim, and Jan Wright, eds. *Contemporary Worship: A Sourcebook for Spirited-Traditional, Praise, and Seeker Services.* Nashville: Abingdon, 1997. Articles and worship services for seeker-sensitive services.

Wuthnow, Robert. *Christianity in the Twenty-First Century: Reflections on the Challenges Ahead.* New York: Oxford University Press, 1995. Discusses the institutional, ethical, doctrinal, political, and cultural challenges facing the church in the new millennium.